D1742297

1 MONTH OF FREE READING

at

www.ForgottenBooks.com

By purchasing this book you are eligible for one month membership to ForgottenBooks.com, giving you unlimited access to our entire collection of over 1,000,000 titles via our web site and mobile apps.

To claim your free month visit:

www.forgottenbooks.com/free834604

ISBN 978-0-260-30612-8
PIBN 10834604

LEWIS ROESCH

Nurseryman

FREDONIA, N.Y.

Special Club and Dealers' Rates,

If $25 or over be remitted, goods in any assortment may be selected from this catalogue at 10 per cent. off lowest rate quoted. If $50 or over, 15 per cent. off. If $75, 20 per cent. If $100 or over, 25 per cent. off.

Vineyardists

Are requested to send a two-cent stamp for samples and circulars of a new and novel grape tie, which is by all odds the best and cheapest thing for tying up grape vines on wire trellises.

Spraying Machinery, Insecticides, and Fungicides.

Parties interested in any of these are invited to send for our new catalogue of these goods. Mailed free.

Our Native Grape.

This work, as described on page 27 of this catalogue, is the latest and best on Grape Culture. It is well worth the publisher's price, $1.50; but in order that we may dispose of a job lot of 800 cloth bound copies previous to April 1st, we offer them at $1.20 each, post-paid. After April 1st at the publisher's price, $1.50 only.

Special Attention.

Is directed to pages 1, 2, 24, 26 and 27 of this catalogue.

The Belt Printing Company, Dunkirk, N. Y.

=:= THIS IS OUR SALESMAN! =:=

He is a hustler and works hard
Day and night for low wages.

His railroad fare costs us but one cent a trip,

His hotel and bar bill nothing,

He will not bore you when you are busy,

But waits patiently until you are ready to listen to him.

He calls now to inform you concerning us and our goods.

1st. What we have to say for ourselves, under oath.

120,000 FRUIT TREES, 135 VARIETIES.
1,200,000 GRAPE VINES, 100 VARIETIES.
900,000 SMALL FRUIT PLANTS, 65 VARIETIES.
6,000 ORNAMENTAL TREES, VINES AND PLANTS.

STATE OF NEW YORK, } ss:
CHAUTAUQUA COUNTY. }

Personally appeared before me Lewis Roesch, who being duly sworn says that he propagated the above mentioned Trees, Vines and Plants for sale, that they are in prime condition, guaranteed strictly true to name and of size and quality represented.

Subscribed and sworn to before me) LEWIS ROESCH,
this 9th day of November, 1894. } Fredonia, N. Y.
F. R. GREEN, Notary Public.)

2nd. What the Press Says.

Extract from the Western Trade Journal, Chicago Ill., of March 27, 1894.

CAN RELY ON RESULTS.

Nurseries Whose Stock is Just as Represented and Whose Methods are Prompt and Honorable.

LEWIS ROESCH, Fredonia, N. Y,

Those of our readers who may have been disappointed in their expectations regarding stock ordered of irresponsible nurseries, and who realize that the best only is good enough in this line, will thank us for calling attention to this trustworthy establishment, whose goods we have found to be identically as represented. It is worthy the patronage of all those who value truthful methods and honest representations, and who would avoid doubtful results.

There is more than the mere money expended to be considered in making choice and purchasing of nursery stock, for it is always too late for correction after imposition is discovered, and unless a responsible house, such as this, is selected, there is no certainty that another year's time has not been lost as well as the money expended thrown away. Hence the necessity of being right before going ahead.

We write only after thorough investigation when we say that the reader is perfectly safe in dealing with these nurseries, for during twenty-one years of journalism we have never come upon more pronounced worth. The stock is first-class in every particular, prices are reasonable, and fair dealing characterizes all transactions. An immense stock and extensive variety to select from is offered, and as the goods are carefully packed and delivered in excellent condition, those who order once, become permanent customers. We advise those who have written us concerning this nursery, or who may be interested in the subject of nursery stock, to obtain price-lists and estimate before purchasing elsewhere. We guarantee satisfactory results.

3rd. What Our Customers Say.

MAGNIFICENT.

LEWIS ROESCH, ESQ. KINGSTON, PA., April 8, 1894.

Dear Sir: The vines you sent me last year were magnificent; I never saw such a mass of roots on young vines before. One vine made a growth of about 11 feet during the season.

Very truly yours, W. L. D.

FREE FROM BLEMISH.

LEWIS ROESCH. MONTICELLO, ILL., April 9th, 1894.

Dear Sir: Your vines are the finest rooted that I ever saw. Everybody pleased. One man said he had to dig a grave to get the roots in straight. Your trees were the smoothest stock, free from blemish, that I have seen here.

Yours truly, W. C. V.

SORRY WE DID NOT ORDER MORE.

MR. LEWIS ROESCH. ANDERSON, IND., April 21, 1894.

Dear Sir: We were very well pleased with the vines and are sorry we did not order more.

Yours truly, S. H. & S.

The New White Gooseberry,

CHAUTAUQUA,

EQUALS THE FINEST AND LARGEST VARIETIES IN SIZE, BEAUTY AND QUALITY, AND EXCELS THEM ALL IN VIGOR AND YIELD.

HISTORY AND DESCRIPTION

The Chautauqua was first found, several years ago, growing in the shade of some plum trees when our attention was attracted to it by the wonderful beauty and size of its fruit and robust habit of bush. We at once sent branches of it in fruit and leaf to noted Horticulturists for identification. Among them was the late Chas Downing, of Newburgh, N. Y. The report from each was that they did not recognize the variety, and that it probably is a seedling of a variety of the English type.

The first plants grown were planted on a warm, gravelly loam in the shade of an apple and peach orchard; excepting a few which were sent to the New York State Experimental Station at Geneva, N. Y., for testing.

So long as the orchard remained, our plants were perfectly healthy and bore annual crops that were the admiration of all beholders. After a few years, however, the trees were removed and then the bushes commenced to mildew. This so discouraged us that we stopped their propagation, supposing all var eties subject to mildew, worthless. However we soon received encouraging reports from the Experimental Station saying that the variety was very valuable in spite of its tendency to mildew. That all varieties of the English type mildewed more or less and that the mildew could be readily overcome by spraying with sulphide of potassium. We tried the remedy and found it quite successful. In fact, we find it but little more expensive than spraying for the potato bug. We also find that other varieties of the English type, and some said to be of American parentage, even, mildew worse than the Chautauqua. However, the place to plant the Chautauqua is in the partial shade afforded by young orchards, where they are not likely to mildew.

The bush of the Chautauqua is a very vigorous, stout, stiff, upright grower, having the usual complement of thorns It should not be planted closer than four by six feet apart. The illustration gives a fair idea of its productiveness. Its leaves are large, glossy and dark green, its fruit is of a beautiful light yellow color perfectly free of spines and hair, veined and translucent, averaging in size 1 to 1¼ inches in diameter, although we have often grown them 1½ inches long. It is rather thick skinned, but very sweet and of exquisite flavor.

The Chautauqua Gooseberry at the World's Fair.

At the World's Fair Exhibition there was perhaps the largest show of gooseberries ever made in this country. The Geneva Experiment Station has planted almost every known variety, both from Europe and America and most of these were on exhibition. In competition with these were two plates of the Chautauqua gooseberry, which overshadowed everything on exhibition, either in the New York State exhibit or in any other exhibit, in size and beauty, and it was equal to anything exhibited in quality. It is safe to say that the Chautauqua is the largest gooseberry ever produced in this country, it is at the same time a remarkably vigorous grower and equally as great a bearer, being the most productive gooseberry in existence.

Report of the New York State Experimental Station-Director Dr. Peter Collier.

GENEVA, N. Y., Aug. 4th, 1893.
Dear Sir:—The Chautauqua gooseberry has been fruited at this Experiment Station for several years. During this time it has been vigorous and productive. The fruit is large, smooth, pale yellow, very good and sweet. It belongs to a class of gooseberries commonly known as English gooseberries, and like the English varieties and their seedlings it sometimes mildews. At this station the mildew has been sucessfully treated for several years by spraying, and the finest English varieties have been kept practically free from this disease. To those who take the trouble to spray their gooseberries we can recommend the Chautaqua as one of the best varieties yet tested on our grounds. Very truly yours.
S. A. BEACH, Horticulturist.

Report of a Former Horticulturist of the New York Experimental Station at Geneva, N. Y.

GENEVA, N. Y., May 14th, 1893.
Dear Sir:—My opinion of your berry (Chautauqua) has not changed and I consider it as good as the best of the English varieties in regard to size of berries and superior to them as to yield and vigor of plant. E. Smith & Sons of this place have watched it for several years and have written you in regard to it. They are business men and would not touch anything of no value.
Yours, etc.,
C. E. HUNN.

Shrewd and Enterprising Business Men Watching the Chautauqua.

The Chase Nurseries, GENEVA, N. Y., Aug. 4, '93.
Dear Sir:—We notice you have rather a fine gooseberry at the Experimental Station. Are you prepared to offer it either by the hundred, thousand, or the entire stock out and out? We would like to hear from you on the subject.
Yours truly,
R. G. CHASE & Co.

E. Smith & Sons, Fruit Growers and Nurserymen,
GENEVA, N. Y., Feb. 14th, 1892.
Sir:—Would like to ascertain what disposition you made of your seedling gooseberry (Chautauqua) that you sent to the Agricultural Experiment Station here for testing. Would you care to dispose of a limited amount of plants for our own cultivation. Awaiting your reply, we remain,
Yours truly,
E. SMITH & SONS.

1000 Plants of the Chautauqua were sold before they were advertised, solely on the strength of what the parties had themselves seen of them.

See price list on page 28.

A PLEA FOR FRUIT.

ONE of the pleasantest of agricultural persuits is Fruit Growing, and withal one of the most profitable also. Fruit of some sort may be grown wherever common farm crops can be raised. There is a demand for it in city and hamlet, lumber and mining camp, on ship-board and for export; fresh, dried and canned. The appetite for it is as universal as that for milk and meat. Fruit is used now where a score of years ago it was unknown, it has become a necessity where then it was deer ad a luxury. Ten times as much is now used as was then. Not a farm or village lot is advertised but what mentions fruit as an inducement, if it has any to boast of. There is not a good thrifty fruit or ornamental tree, vine, or shrub on any place, but what increases its value four to ten times what it cost to raise it. Then why not grow fruit to improve your home-stead? Plenty to eat, to give away, and to sell. Too much trouble did you say? Can buy it cheaper? Why then not give your son John or Henry half an acre of ground to grow it for you, you to pay him conscientiously whatever it would cost in the market? You might do worse. Many a large and profitable business has been started in this way, and many a mortgage lifted which grain growing or dairying were unable to raise.

Conditions of Success.—Fruit culture depends for success or the same conditions as ordinary farming. These are mainly liberal fertilizing, a careful preparation of ground, proper care and culture at the right time, and a judicious selection of varieties suited to the soil, climate, purpose and market. First of importance for fruit growing is a dry soil. Ground too wet for winter wheat should be under drained, unless plowing it up into narrow lands with deep dead-furrows between be sufficient.

What and When to Plant.—Plant mainly of varieties that are generally successful and such as do best in your own neighborhood, but do not confine yourself to them alone. Try other well recommended kinds and new varieties. Be enterprising. If you are the first in a community who learns of the merits of a new kind you may get more satisfaction and money out of a small lot of them than you would out of a large lot of common kinds. Select, principally, varieties of robust constitution that are hardy, healthy, good growers and bearers, for of what avail is high quality, beauty and size, if they bear little or not at all on account of feeble growth and health?

Preparation of Ground.—Pulverize the soil thoroughly at least twelve inches deep. Plow sod ground early enough to become thoroughly rotten before planting. But if not practical to do so, then plow into lands the width of rows and plant into the dead furrows. Harrow ground thoroughly to make surface soil mellow, with which to cover the roots. Excellent results are often obtained in this way. If coarse manure is applied it should be plowed in. But well rotted manure is much better and should only be harrowed in so as to remain near the surface. Of commercial fertilizers unleached hard wood ashes are best, especially on warm soil. Next best is bone dust.

Planting Trees.—Stake the ground out into straight rows both ways, driving a stake two feet long where the trees are to stand. Dig the holes wide and deep enough to hold the roots without crowding or bending, and keep driving the stake down so it will stand where first put, when the hole is dug. Cut smoothly all broken or bruised roots back to sound wood. Prune each shoot, forming the top, back to one bud. During the summer rub off all buds that start along the body except five or six that may be wanted for a top. Plant same depth as the tree stood in the nursery, or a trifle deeper, always on the same side of the stake, and in the same manner as recommended for grape vines. The distance trees are planted apart should be regulated by the quality of soil, thrift of variety, etc. A strong growing variety on rich soil under thorough cultivation, will grow larger and needs proportionately more room than a poor grower on poor soil. Peach trees may be planted between apple trees each way to good advantage, requiring three times as many peach trees as apple. By the time the apple trees need the room the peaches will be past their prime and may be removed. Dwarf pears may be planted among Standards in the same way, or the same may be filled up with small fruits as strawberries, currants, and especially gooseberries, to which a partial shade seems beneficial.

Overbearing is a prolific source of poor fruit, as well as weakness, disease and death to fruit trees, shrubs and vines. This is principally on account of the tax on their vitality by the bearing of seed. Two thousand fruits on a tree, measuring five bushels, are worth much less in market, while they tax the tree twice as much as one thousand fruits would, measuring the same number of bushels. Every fruit grower, ambitious of success, will heroically remove, when about half grown all, beyond what the tree ought to bear, consistent with good fruit, health and crop, leaving, of course, the best.

Care of Stock When Received.—When the stock arrives unpack and plant at once. Should it, however, appear frozen, do not unpack, but cover it up in a cool, dark cellar, or other convenient place where it may thaw out gradually. Freezing does not injure plants, but rapid thawing with exposure to light and air does. If not ready to plant when received, heel them in, in a dry place, protected both against sun and sweeping winds. Dig a trench deep enough to hold the vines, plants or trees, open the bundles and spread them out against the side of the trench an inch or two thick; cover them with a layer of soil, which press firmly against the roots to exclude air, put on another layer of stock and soil, etc., until completed, taking great care to keep the different varieties separate and well labeled. If the vines and plants are to be left heeled in over winter, both root and top must be well covered with earth, and over that place a cover of coarse horse manure and other litter to insure safety. Trees are heeled in leaning with prevailing wind at an angle of 30 or 40 degrees, and buried one-third to one-half of their length. The balance may be covered with evergreen boughs or other brush, but nothing that would attract mice.

Parties desiring further information on the subject of fruit growing are referred to the list of Horticultural publications mentioned on **page 27.**

Selection of Varieties.—Beginners in grape culture are often puzzled as to what to select from among the multitude of varieties offered. To such we would say that climatic conditions and other circumstances generally so limit the planter in his selection that he has usually but a comparatively small number to select from, and often too few indeed. In the extreme North the seasons are short, and winters severe, so that none but the earliest and hardiest varieties succeed. In sections where the best can be grown nothing else is wanted. For family use, only the best that can be well grown are desirable; for market, the most profitable only. What those are each particular locality and market must determine. The most profitable in one locality and market may or may not be so in another. For keeping and distant shipping, tough skinned varieties are preferable. In sections where grapes are much subject to mildew and rot, only the most robust and healthy should be selected.

Varieties of the Labrusca class, to which belongs the Concord, succeed over a larger extent of territory than any other, and are particularly recommended for planting in the North and North-west. To this class belong the new varieties, Early Victor, Eaton, Hayes, Jewell, Lady, Leader, Moore's Diamond, Moore's Early, Moyer, Niagara, Pocklington, Vergennes, Worden, etc. Varieties of the Riparia class, such as Elvira, Etta, Missouri Riessling, etc., seem better adapted to the South and Southwest. Hybrids containing foreign blood as Agawam, Downing, Wilder, etc., are not as reliable as some other varieties, being more or less subject to rot and mildew in unfavorable localities and seasons, yet they are of the best for all purposes where they do succeed. Large to very large in bunch and berry, good keepers and shippers, strong growers, productive and of the best quality. Varieties we cannot recommend have been omitted from the descriptive part of this catalogue, but as we still have some vines, and more or less call for them, we keep them in price list.

New Varieties.—Not all new varieties that are being constantly introduced are improvements, but many of them are, and some prove to be magnificent triumphs of horticulture, to know which is well worth a trial of them all. In this age of close competition it becomes necessary for the fruit grower, if he would make the most of his opportunities, to make himself at once thoroughly acquainted with all varieties that are at all suitable for his locality. To which end he will give each kind a fair trial in a small way as fast as it is introduced and then plant largely of such as he discovers to be most desirable and profitable. It is our practice to subject each and every candidate for public favor to a trial on our own grounds and to freely give the result to everyone interested. This, however, though valuable in a general way, cannot take the place of a trial on everyone's own grounds, for the reason that a variety which may prove hardy here, may not be so in another section having a severer climate or in a location of greater exposure, or one tender here may be hardy enough in a milder climate or more protected situation. Again, a variety that is subject to mildew here may be more or less so in other places. *A trial on the spot only can fully settle such matters*

Planting.—Strong growing varieties as Concord, Niagara, Rogers Hybrids, etc., should be planted 8 to 10 feet apart each way, and weaker growers as Delaware, Lady, Jessica, etc., some 6 to 8 feet, according to the strength and quality of the soil. In cold climates and exposed situation plant deeper than in warm ones, to avoid injury by severe freezing. For same reason plant deeper in a loose soil than in a compact one. If the soil is clayey or wet, plant some seven or ten inches deep, and in the fall plow up to them, leaving a dead furrow between the rows to carry off the water But if the ground be dry and gravely or sandy, plant them not less than twelve to fifteen inches deep. While planting the vines use care not to let the roots get dry. Cut them back to about a foot long and dig a hole large enough so the roots can be spread out in it, about as they grow in the nursery. Work good, rich, fine and moist surface soil around and amongst the roots until they are all covered when they should be firmly tramped down. Cover up but partially at first and level off gradually during the season. After planting trim vines back to within two or three buds of the ground.

Pruning.—The object of pruning is to grow the greatest amount of fruit of the best quality, and at the same time canes enough and no more than to produce an equally good crop the next year. If grape vines are not sufficiently pruned they bear much more fruit than they are able to perfect. The result is they overbear, often to their permanent injury. The fruit is so small, scragly and late as to be next to worthless, besides they fail to grow and ripen canes strong enough to bear a good crop the next season. By proper pruning you concentrate the vigor of a vine into a smaller number of canes and clusters, which it can perfect. The berries and clusters grow large and ripen early, thus you secure a greater number of pounds of fruit to the vine (though less clusters) of much superior quality, and at the same time strong, well ripened canes for the next year's bearing, and all this without any injury to the vine whatever. If vines do not grow strong enough, cultivate better, fertilize and trim close. If too strong and do not bear enough, give them more room, either by building the trellis higher or by cutting out every second or third vine. Prune the remaining ones longer so as to cover the space.

Summer Pruning.—This is intended to supplement winter pruning. It is done as soon as the new shoots get to be five or six inches long (early in June here) and consists in breaking off all new shoots that neither show flower buds nor are needed for the next season's bearing canes. All further pruning during the summer is harmful.

How to Prune.—The first fall after planting, cut the vines back to the ground again, leaving but a spur of three or four buds above ground. Let two canes grow the second season. They ought now to make a growth of from five to eight feet, if so, cut one of them back to three buds in the fall following, and the other to within three or four feet, to bear. Should they have made a larger growth more may be left, if less, but little if any. For if the vine is not strong enough to force a good growth of wood, it is too weak to bear fruit. As the vines grow older and stronger, from three to five canes may be left to bear (always preferring those that start within a foot of the root), and these trained out in fan shape on stakes or trellises. Two or more year old wood ought always be cut down as much as possible, as it is the young wood only that bears fruit. This mode of trimming and training is called the fan system. But there are many others, the description of which is not within the scope of this catalogue. Whatever system be adopted, the treatment the first two years is practically the same. Grape vines may be trained against buildings, fences or on stakes and trellises. Wire trellises some five feet high are the best for vineyards. All young vines should be protected, at least the first winter or two, by plowing up to them, or otherwise covering them with soil. The pruning may be done any time after the leaves fall in the autumn and before the sap starts in the spring, although a little bleeding will do them no harm.

Yield.—In ordinary vineyard culture from two to four tons per acre, and from five to fifteen pounds per vine, according to variety, is a fair average yield. However, six to eight tons per acre are sometimes produced and single vines have been known to yield bushels of fruit.

DESCRIPTIVE LIST.

See price list on page 28.

Agawam—(Rogers No. 15.) A large, red grape ripening with the Concord. Sweet and of a rich, aromatic flavor. A rank grower and very productive. One of the most reliable of Rogers Hybrids.

Aminia—(Rogers No. 39.) A beautiful black grape ripening before the Concord. Bunch large and compact, berry very large. Sweet and excellent flavor. Productive and valuable for garden and vineyard.

Barry—(Rogers No. 43.) Black. Ripens before Concord. Bunch very large and shouldered. Berry large, flesh tender, flavor sweet and good. Vine vigorous, healthy and hardy. A beautiful grape.

Berkman's—New, red. A cross between Clinton and Delaware, originated in S. C. Much like the Clinton in vigor, health and hardiness of vines. In color, quality and appearance of fruit it is similar to the Delaware and ripens about the same time.

Brighton—New, dark red. Ripens with, or before Delaware. Bunch large, long and shouldered, berries medium, skin thin, flesh tender, sweet and best quality. Vine vigorous and fairly productive. It yields best if planted between other varieties. A valuable and desirable grape for garden and vineyard.

BRIGHTON. ¼ size.

Catawba—Well known, red. Bunch and berry large and of a rich vinous, refreshing flavor, and best quality. Ripens several weeks after Concord.

Centennial—New. Color green, with blush in the sun. Bunch large, long, and shouldered ; berries medium ; flesh very sweet and juicy and of exquisite quality. Skin thin but tough ; a good keeper ; vine vigorous, healthy and hardy Liable to overbear ; prune short. Very desirable for home use. Its poor color spoils it for market.

Champion—(or Talman) A prolific and profitable early market grape ; black ; quality only second to third rate. Ripens with or before Moore's Early. Flesh sweet, juicy and foxy ; a rank grower, very healthy, hardy and productive.

Clinton—Black ; desirable for wine and preserving ; bunch and berry small to medium ; flesh juicy and spicy ; colors up with the Concord but is not ripe until two or three weeks later. A rank grower and hardy.

Concord—The most extensively planted and generally successful grape in America. Black, bunch and berry large, fair quality, medium early ; vine a rank grower, very healthy, hardy and productive.

Cottage—A seedling of Concord, a little smaller in bunch and berry, but more compact ; sweeter and a few days earlier ; not quite as productive. A rank grower, very healthy and hardy.

Cynthiana—Highly prized for wine at the South and Southwest. Bunch medium, berries small, sweet, black ; vigorous and healthy ; late.

Delaware—The standard of excellence. Red ; ripens with or before Concord. Bunch and berry medium, compact, flesh juicy, very sweet and refreshing ; vine very hardy and productive ; a slow grower, requires rich soil, good culture and close pruning. Subject to mildew in poor grape sections and seasons.

Diana—Red ; ripens soon after Concord. Sweet and high flavored ; bunch medium, short and compact ; berry medium. Good keeper and shipper ; vine vigorous and fairly productive.

Dracut Amber—A very early red grape. Large in bunch and berry ; sweet but foxy ; hardy, healthy, vigorous and productive ; valuable for the extreme North.

Duchess—White. Ripens soon after Concord. Berry medium, clusters medium to large, compact, long and shouldered. In flavor and quality of the best. Usually hardy and free from disease. A stong grower and productive ; also an excellent keeper and shipper.

Early Ohio—New, black. Originated near Cleveland, O. Ripens a week before Moore's Early, and is of better quality. Bunch large, berry medium and of a spicy, pleasant flavor. Adheres persistently to the stem. A strong, robust, healthy grower, hardy and very productive. A profitable market variety.

Early Victor—Black. Ripens early, before Concord and of better quality ; of medium size in bunch and berry ; sweet, pleasant and not foxy. Vine a strong grower ; healthy, hardy and productive.

EATON. Reduced size.

Eaton—New, black. Originated by John B. Moore of Mass. A seedling of Concord. Bunch large and berry very large. About as early, but not as sweet as its parent. Pleasant, juicy, with tender pulp. Vine vigorous, healthy and productive.

Elvira—White. Ripens about with Catawba; a very strong, healthy and robust grower, and as productive as anything we have seen yet. Bunch and berry of medium size and very compact. Highly prized as a wine grape at the South.

Empire State—A white grape of first rate quality, ripening about a week after Concord. Bunch long but slender. Berries medium, sweet. juicy and sprightly. Free from fox, skin thin but tough, a good keeper. The vine is a vigorous grower, quite healthy and fairly hardy.

Essex—(Rog. No. 41.) Black; ripens with Concord. Medium sized bunch of very large berries, tender, sweet and of an aromatic flavor; healthy, vigorous and productive.

Etta—New, white. A seedling of Elvira which it resembles but has larger berries and firmer skin, and is less compact and of better quality. The vine is of vigorous growth, healthy, hardy and very productive. Late.

Gaertner—(Rog. No. 14.) Early, red; medium to large in bunch and berry; sweet, rich and aromatic.

Geneva—New, white. Said to be of ironclad hardiness, a strong, robust, healthy grower. Ripens about with Concord, of medium size in bunch and berry; quality fine; skin thick; a good keeper and shipper.

Goethe—(Rog. No. 1.) Light red, bunch large, berries very large, flesh sweet and juicy; ripens about with Catawba. Vine vigorous, rank grower and generally healthy. Good keeper; highly esteemed at the South for table and wine.

Green Mountain—New, white. Originated in Vermont. It is said to be as early as Moore's Early. Bunch long but slender, berry medium, sweet and of fine quality. It is inclined to drop its berries when ripe.

Hartford—Black; ripens from four to six days before Concord; bunch and berry large, flesh sweet, but somewhat foxy; inclined to drop its berries when fully ripe. Vigorous, healthy and very prolific.

Hayes—White. Originated by John B. Moore of Mass. Ripens a week before Concord. Bunch and berry medium, skin firm. flesh tender, very sweet, juicy and excellent. Vine hardy and healthy, similar to Martha, both in growth and fruit, of better quality, but not so productive.

Herbert—(Rogers No. 44.) Black; bunch and berry large, flesh sweet, tender and of good quality. Early, hardy and productive. One of the best of Roger's Hybrids.

Highland—New, black. A strong grower, healthy, and very productive; bunch and berry very large and handsome; ripens with or soon after Catawba. Quality very good. Desirable wherever it will ripen.

Iona—A red grape of the best quality; ripens before Catawba; is not reliable and cannot be recommended for extensive vineyard planting.

Isabella—A well known old variety; black; bunch and berries large and of good quality. Strong grower and productive, but late and not very hardy.

Ives—Black, colors up early but does not get fully ripe until after the Concord. Bunch and berry medium; compact. Quality fairly good when fully ripe. Very healthy, hardy, vigorous and productive. A generally successful market grape.

Jefferson—A red grape of the best quality; bunch very large and handsome, berries medium; vine vigorous, healthy and productive. Ripens with or before Catawba.

Jessica—A new white grape, originated in Canada. Ripens with the earliest; small to medium in bunch and berry. Sweet as honey, not foxy. Vine a fair, compact grower; hardy, healthy and productive.

Jewell—New black. Much like Early Victor in appearance and quality, but earlier; bunch and berry medium, sweet and sprightly, good, without a trace of fox; skin thin but tough; vine vigorous, hardy, healthy and productive and has never been known to either rot or mildew.

Lady—White; an excellent early grape; healthy, hardy and productive, but a slow grower; should be grown on rich soil, or else closely planted and trimmed. Bunch and berry large, compact, handsome and of good quality.

Lady Washington—New white. A handsome grape of good quality; berry large, bunch very large, double shouldered and of a fine yellow color; vine a rank grower and productive; fairly healthy and hardy. Ripens a little before Catawba.

MOORE'S EARLY. ¼ size.

Leader—New white. Originated in Ohio. A vine of robust constitution, a strong grower and very hardy, healthy and productive; medium in bunch and berry and very sweet. Ripens early.

Lindley—(Rogers No. 9). A red grape of the best quality, and one of the most desirable of Rogers Hybrids. Ripens with Concord and keeps well; medium to large in bunch and berry; flesh tender, sweet and of high aromatic flavor. Vine vigorous, hardy and healthy. It seems to be more productive when mixed with other varieties.

Martha—White; ripens with Concord, of which it is a seedling; medium in bunch and berry; color greenish, turning yellow when dead ripe. Good as Concord in quality, but sweeter. A good grower and bearer; hardy and healthy.

Massasoit—(Rogers No. 3). Red; bunch and berry large; flesh tender, sweet and pulpless, with agreeable aroma. The earliest of Rogers Hybrids, ripens with Hartford. Vine vigorous, healthy, hardy and fairly productive.

Merrimac—(Rogers No. 19). Black; ripens about with the Concord; bunch and berry very large; quality good; very similar to Wilder but hardier. Strong grower and productive.

Mills—New black. Described as a cross between the Creveling and a foreign variety. Bunch very large, compact and shouldered. Berry large and adheres firmly to the stem. Flesh firm, meaty, juicy, rich and sprightly. Vine vigorous, healthy and productive. Ripens soon after Concord and is a good keeper. Promising.

Missouri Riessling—(Grein's No. 1). A white wine grape, ripens before Catawba; bunch and berry of medium size and good quality. Vine very vigorous, healthy, hardy and productive.

Moore's Early—Black; a seedling of the Concord, which it resembles. Equal to it in quality, health and hardiness, but ripening some ten days earlier. It is a good, fair grower and bearer, but requires age to do its best. Bunch large, berry very large. It is being extensively planted for market; valuable for garden and vineyard.

Moore's Diamond—New; white. A strong grower and quite healthy and hardy. Very productive. Bunch and berry large. Quality fine. Ripens a little before Concord. Very desirable for both domestic and market purposes.

Moyer—This new grape originated in Canada, and seems to be a cross between the Delaware and some purely native variety. In hardiness, quality, color and size it is the equal of the Delaware, but is a better grower, two weeks earlier (ripening with the Champion) and has so far been free from rot and mildew. Very valuable.

MOORE'S DIAMOND. Reduced size.

Niagara—A magnificent white grape and very valuable for both garden and vineyard; a rank grower and very productive of beautiful bunches of the largest size. Berries large, with a tough skin; quality good. Ripens about with Concord. Popular with vineyardists and amateurs North and South.

Norwood—New, black; large, of good quality, vigorous, healthy, productive. Suitable for the amateur only. Ripens with or soon after the Concord.

Norton's Virginia—A black wine grape. Highly esteemed at the South. Ripens late; bunch long, berries small; a rank grower, healthy and productive.

Perkins—Pale red. Ripens before Concord; bunch medium, berry large, sweet and juicy, but foxy. Vine a rank grower, healthy, hardy and productive.

Pocklington—This is becoming more popular every year as a valuable market grape, it being so large and showy in both bunch and berry. Compact and of a beautiful golden color. Quality about as good as the Concord, with which it ripens, by some liked even better. Vine vigorous and very healthy, hardy and productive.

Prentiss—A white variety of good quality; bunch and berry medium to large, compact, vigorous and very productive; keeps well. Rather late and tender.

Rochester—A red grape of high quality; ripening early. Bunch very large and compact; berries medium, very sweet rich and aromatic. Inclined to overbear. Prune short.

POCKLINGTON. ¼ size.

Salem—(Rogers 22). One of the most popular of Rogers Hybrids. Red, ripens with Concord; bunch and berry large, flesh sweet, tender, with a rich, fine flavor. A good keeper, vigorous and productive.

Telegraph—Black. Ripens with Hartford. Vine a strong grower, healthy and very productive; bunch large, very compact and showy; berry medium. Flavor pleasant and sprightly.

Triumph—New. A white grape of very large size and fine quality, but late. Is thought highly of in the South.

Ulster Prolific—A very desirable new red variety. Originated in New York State. Medium in bunch and berry, skin thin but tough. Very sweet and of exquisite flavor. It ripens with the Concord; keeps and carries well. The vine is very hardy, healthy, vigorous and productive. An acquisition.

Victoria—White, of good size and quality, very vigorous, healthy, hardy, productive and reliable. Highly recommended by the Rural New Yorker. The best out of 1,500 seedlings grown by the late T. B. Miner of N. J.

Vergennes—Red; ripens with or soon after Concord; bunch of medium size, berry large, skin thick and tough. Vine very vigorous, healthy and productive, hardy; quality excellent; a splendid keeper and shipper.

Wilder—(Rogers No. 4). Black, bunch and berry very large, flesh sweet, pleasant and of excellent flavor. Vine a good grower, healthy and productive; ripens soon after Concord. A popular market grape and good keeper and shipper.

Woodruff Red—A new grape of ironclad hardiness. A rank grower and very healthy. The fruit is large in bunch and berry, attractive, shouldered, sweet and of fair quality, but somewhat foxy. Desirable as a market variety where many others fail. It ripens soon after Concord.

Worden—This excellent grape has come to the front by merit alone. It is as hardy, healthy, vigorous and productive as the Concord, of which it is a seedling, but better in quality, sweeter, larger in bunch and berry and several days earlier. The worst that can be said of it is, that it will crack under conditions that the Concord will. Very valuable for garden and vineyard.

Wyoming Red—A very early red grape; desirable for garden and vineyard. A good grower, very healthy and hardy; bunch and berry medium. Sweet, but a little foxy.

See price list on page 28.

The growing of this fruit and the gooseberry is the easiest and least troublesome of any the fruit grower has to deal with. About the only thing to do is to keep the weeds down and to gather the crop, which latter process does not demand that close attention necessary for other berries. This fruit may be left to hang a week or two after ripe, if necessary, without any harm. They are usually gathered when pickers are not busy with raspberries. Plant in rows about five or six feet apart and three feet in the row. On the red and white varieties the fruit is mainly borne on the wood two years old, the black varieties on wood one year old. Prune accordingly. To kill worms on currant and gooseberry bushes, dust them with white hellebore while the dew is on.

Yield.—About one hundred and fifty bushels per acre and some two or three quarts per bush, but often a great deal more.

Cherry—Old and tried. Very popular in market on account of its great size and deep red color. Not as productive as others.

Crandall—New, black. A seedling of the Mo. wild currant, exceedingly productive, a rank grower, thoroughly hardy, and free from insect enemies and disease. The fruit is of the largest size, is free from that rank odor of other black currants, has a peculiar flavor of its own, and is as eatable off hand as the huckleberry which it resembles. But its greatest usefulness is for culinary purposes, being unexcelled for pies, jams, and jellies,

Fay's Prolific—New. As large as the Cherry, with longer clusters, much more productive and better quality. A great improvement over the old varieties.

La Versailles—Red. Nearly as large as the Cherry, much more productive and not quite as acid. Very profitable.

Lee's Prolific—New, black. This variety is larger, more productive, sweeter and of better quality than any of the old black varieties.

Red Dutch—Very productive, good quality, but small.

Victoria—A strong grower and very productive of bright red berries on very long clusters. Very late and profitable.

White Grape—Large, mild, of excellent quality and productive. Best of the white varieties for home use and market.

GOOSEBERRIES.

See price list on page 28.

The Gooseberry is a rank grower and generally needs more trimming than the currant, otherwise its culture is about the same. It is usually picked just as it commences to ripen.

The fruit is used for pies, tarts, canning, etc., and can be shipped in boxes and barrels as well as in crates.

They accommodate themselves better to shady situations than any other fruit; indeed, partial shade seems to be just what they require. The demand for this fruit is not so great as that for other berries, but it is growing fast. Six to eight quarts per bush is a fair crop, but we have grown as many as three pecks on a bush of the Houghton.

Downing—The largest of the American varieties. Whitish green, and of good quality; the bush is a strong, stout, upright grower, and quite prolific and healthy.

Houghton Seedling—Pale red, medium sized berries, of good quality. A vigorous but slender grower, healthy and very productive.

DOWNING.

Industry.—Very large, dark red and of a rich, pleasant flavor, but not of robust constitution.

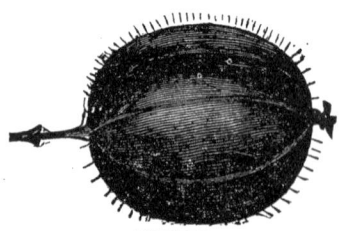

INDUSTRY.

Smith's Improved—Large, yellow, skin thin. Of best quality and unsurpassed for table use and cooking. A good grower and free from mildew.

RASPBERRIES.

See price list on page 29.

KANSAS.

For garden culture, raspberries may be planted about four feet apart each way and tied up to stakes. A row or two each of Blackberries, Raspberries, Grapes, Currants, Gooseberries and Strawberries across the garden will be very convenient to attend to and would be a perpetual source of pleasure, comfort, health and profit all through the season.

For field culture plant in rows six or seven feet apart and two and one-half to three feet in the row, and set two to five inches deep, according to the nature of the soil. In the fall or spring following trim the canes back to within one or two feet of the crown, according to the growth they have made. About in June, when the young canes have made a growth of from one and a half to two feet high, pinch off the tip ends to make them throw out laterals. This makes them stocky and able to resist high winds. After fruiting remove all the old wood as the new canes need all the room, and should have all the strength the root is able to furnish.

Red Raspberries usually produce many more canes than are desirable for fruiting purposes, only four or five of them should be left to grow in a hill and the rest hoed off as soon as they appear, the same as weeds.

Yield—A bush is able to bear several quarts, but about two thousand quarts per acre is a fair average yield under ordinary field culture.

RED RASPBERRIES.

Cuthbert—The best late red raspberry for home use and market. Fruit bright red and very large; bush very vigorous, hardy and prolific. Very valuable.

Golden Queen—New, similar to the Cuthbert (of which it is a seedling), except in color, which is what its name implies. Very large, hardy, vigorous and productive. No garden should be without it.

Marlboro—A new variety that has come to stay. A very large, bright red berry, ripening with the earliest, firm and of good quality. Very hardy and a great grower and bearer.

Philadelphia—A strong grower, suckers less than any other; exceedingly productive; berries dark red, of good size and fair quality.

Thompson's Early Prolific—The earliest of all. Plant is a strong grower, very robust, healthy, hardy and productive. Fruit of a remarkable bright crimson color, large, firm and good.

MARLBORO.

BLACK RASPBERRIES.

Doolittle—A very popular early variety, valuable for home use, market and drying.

Gregg—Very large and late. Bush a strong upright grower, productive and very desirable for market and home use.

Johnston's Sweet—New, early as Souhegan, nearly as large as the Gregg, coal black and firm. Sweeter and of better quality than any other blackcap. The bush is of strong upright growth, entirely hardy and very productive.

Kansas—New. Originated in Kansas where it is prized as the best Black Cap. Ripens early and is as large or larger than the Gregg. Jet black, firm, handsome and of best quality. Very vigorous and productive.

Ohio—Very productive and firm, season medium to late. Bush strong grower and hardy. Very valuable for shipping and drying.

Palmer's Seedling—A new variety of great promise. Very early and ripens its whole crop in a short time. A strong grower, great bearer and very hardy. Berries large and good. It always commands the highest price in market.

Schaeffer's Colossal—Colossal both in bush and size of berry. A good shipper, excellent to dry and unsurpassed for canning. Dark red and of fine quality. The bush does not sucker but roots from the tips only. Very productive.

Souhegan—Early, hardy and productive. Sweet and of fine quality. Not very firm.

Winona—New. Early as Souhegan, large as Gregg, firm, strong grower, very hardy and productive.

BLACKBERRIES.

See price list on page 29.

The culture of the Blackberry is essentially the same as that of the Raspberry, except as it is a stronger bush it needs a little more room and longer trimming. The introduction of the hardy Snyder some years ago awakened much interest in the culture of this delicious fruit in the North and North-west. Since then a number of equally hardy and improved varieties have been introduced, by the planting of which as good and large fruit may now be grown in Minnesota as in New Jersey.

Average yield about one hundred bushels per acre, or two or three quarts to the bush.

Ancient Briton—New. This variety was brought from England a few years ago and unostentatiously and by merit alone has it worked itself into the esteem of both growers and consumers. It is very hardy, vigorous, healthy and exceedingly productive of the very largest berries. Late.

Early Harvest—New Very early, of medium size, productive but is not quite hardy.

EARLY HARVEST.

Erie—New. Originated on the shore of Lake Erie and is of ironclad hardiness, having endured 25 degrees below zero unprotected and unharmed. Superior in size and productiveness to all others; of strong growth and free from rust and other diseases, second only to Early Harvest in earliness, of uniform size and shape, firm and of excellent quality. A great acquisition.

ERIE.

Kittatiny—A rank grower and productive, nearly hardy here. Berries large and good.

Lucretia Dewberry—The Dewberry is a running or trailing blackberry, and may be left to sprawl on the ground or else tied up on stakes or trellises like grape vines. They propagate from the tips like black raspberries and never sucker. Prune severely. The Lucretia is new and the best of its class, ripening before any blackberry. Very large and wonderfully productive and of the very best quality. Entirely hardy, but even if it were not, its trailing habit makes it very easy of protection.

Minnewaski—New. Resembling Kittatiny but ripens very early, and is healthy and hardy. Fruit large and fine quality.

Snyder—Very popular on account of its great hardiness and productiveness. Berries are of medium size, sweet and good. Reliable.

Stone's Hardy—The hardiest of the well tried varieties. Equal in size, quality and productiveness to the Snyder, but later.

TAYLOR'S PROLIFIC.

Taylor's Prolific—Medium to large, tender and sweet; a strong grower, productive and quite hardy.

Wachusett's Thornless—A medium sized berry of the best quality. The bush is quite hardy, productive and nearly thornless. Very desirable.

Wilson's Early—This is the great market berry of New Jersey. Fruit is very large and early. Bush tender, and needs protection at the North.

Wilson Jr.—A seedling of, and a great improvement over Wilson's Early. Larger, earlier, hardier, and much more productive. Not subject to rust.

STRAWBERRIES.

See price list on page 29.

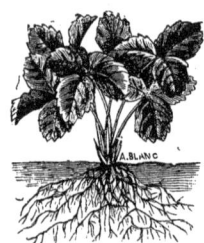

For home use, strawberries may be planted in rows some three feet apart and one foot in the row. But much larger and more fruit can be grown by closer planting, say one by one and a half feet, cutting off the runners as fast as they grow. In field culture they are usually planted in rows four feet apart and one foot in the row and runners left to grow. Planted so, most of the cultivation may be done with horse labor. It is very essential that they be kept free of weeds all through the season. It is well to mulch them early in the winter for protection against severe and sudden changes of weather, and to keep them from heaving out. Coarse horse manure is first-rate for this purpose, but in want of it, potato tops, corn stalks, evergreen boughs, or other litter having no weed seeds in, will do. Coarse material has to be removed in the spring, while the finer parts of horse manure may be left to fertilize and keep the ground damp, which is quite an advantage in dry weather. We cannot recommend summer planting in the North, as the plants are then very young, tender and expensive and the weather unfavorable. Whatever the heat and dry weather does not destroy, a severe winter is sure to. Early spring is a far better time. In the South, where winters are mild, late fall and winter is no doubt the best time to plant. Varieties marked P have imperfect blossoms and to produce well should have every third or fourth row of some variety, not so marked, planted between them, then they are even more productive than those having perfect blossoms.

Yield.—A fair average crop, under ordinary field culture, is about one hundred bushels per acre, but much more than this has been grown, even as much as a quart per plant.

Bidwell—One of the most desirable. Early, very large, productive and of fine flavor. Plant is a strong, rapid grower and hardy.

Bubach's No. 5. P—New. This is one of the very best varieties for home use or near by market. The plant is very large, dark green. Very hardy, robust and productive. Fruit of the largest size and uniform. Early; continues a long time in bearing.

BUBACH'S NO. 5.

Cloud, P—This is one of the earliest and best market berries of the South. It is a very vigorous, healthy and robust grower and very productive of fine, large fruit.

Crawford—New. Is very large and firm, of even shape and beautiful color. No white ends. The plant is a robust and luxuriant grower, large and stocky, free from rust and is very productive.

Crescent Seedling, P—One of the rankest growers, and a

CRAWFORD.

great bearer of medium to large-sized nice looking berries. Fair quality, but soft.

Cumberland Triumph—For home use and near market this is one of the best. Very large size, even, regular shape and very attractive. A strong grower and productive.

Gandy—The best late berry. A robust grower, healthy and hardy. The fruit is very large, firm and of bright crimson color.

Haverland—A cross between Crescent and Sharpless. The fruit is of large, uniform shape, beautiful color and excellent flavor. Plants are large, robust, healthy and ripen the fruit up early.

Jessie—New. This is not the largest Strawberry we have ever seen, nor the prettiest, firmest, most productive nor best grower, but it combines all these good qualities in a high degree and is very desirable for both field and garden.

James Vick—A rank grower, very hardy, and in productiveness not excelled by any other. Berries medium to large size, very firm and of good quality. Needs a strong soil to perfect the enormous load of fruit it sets.

Kentucky—One of the old reliable and generally successful berries. Large and of the latest to ripen. Plant very robust, hardy and productive.

Lady Rusk—New. Originated in Illinois and is said to be superior to any other variety for market purposes owing to its good carrying and handling qualities. It is a rank grower. Very productive, of good size, very hardy and healthy.

Michael's Early—Resembles Crescent in vigor, health and fruit, but is much earlier.

Miner's Prolific—A large, dark red berry of fine quality and very productive. Firm and robust. Desirable.

Mount Vernon—An excellent berry for home use and market, ripening late. It blooms late, thereby often escaping spring frosts when others are nipped. Fruit very large and of excellent quality. Plant robust, hardy and very productive.

Sharpless—Very popular. Berries of immense size, of cockscomb shape. Good quality and moderately firm, a strong grower and productive. To do its best it should be planted on strong ground and kept in hills.

Warfield, P—New. The best market and shipping berry. A rank, hardy grower: more productive and larger than Crescent, of a dark red glossy color and equally as firm as Wilson. Season medium.

Wilson's Albany—This old variety occupies the same place among strawberries that the Concord does among grapes. Its great firmness makes it especially popular with shippers.

ASPARAGUS.

See price list on page 29.

The culture of this early and delicious vegetable is usually very profitable. It comes early in the season when there is little else to market and the proceeds are very acceptable. It is a rank feeder and must be manured very highly. Plow or spade the ground at least a foot deep, work in and mix with the soil thoroughly, plenty of rich, well-rotted manure. For field culture plant in rows three and one-half or four feet apart, and one or one and one-half feet apart in the row. But for home use they may be planted one and one-half feet apart each way and some three inches deep. Keep the ground clear of weeds, and spread on a good coat of rich manure every fall.

Conover's Colossal—Large, a strong grower, productive and of fine quality.

Palmetto—New, earlier, larger and more productive than the above.

Barr's Mammoth—New, earliest of all, otherwise the equal of Conover's.

RHUBARB OR PIE PLANT.

See price list on page 29.

The first thing in spring to furnish material for pie and sauce. Also very desirable for canning and should be in every garden. Plant three or four feet apart and make the soil rich. The richer the soil the earlier, larger and better the stalks will be.

Myatt's Linnæus—Early and good.   **Victoria**—The largest and best.

APPLES.

See price list on page 29.

Plant apple trees 30 to 40 feet apart each way. Russian varieties are marked by affixing an "R" to name. Dwarf apple trees we can furnish only of such varieties as have a "D" after the name.

SUMMER.

Early Harvest.—Medium to large, pale yellow, mild and excellent; productive. August.

Red Astrachan. D.—Large and handsome, crimson, rather acid; a good grower and very hardy. Aug.

Sweet Bough.—Large, pale yellow, sweet, tender and juicy; a moderate grower; productive; profitable. Aug.

Tetofski. R. D.—Medium size, yellow, striped red; juicy, sprightly and very attractive. July and Aug.

Yellow Transparent. R.—New, medium, pale yellow; tender, juicy, sprightly; a good early bearer. Aug.

AUTUMN.

Alexander. R.—Very large and handsome, crimson; sub-acid, pleasant. Sept. and Oct.

BIETIGHEIMER. ¼ size.

Bietigheimer. D.—One of the largest and handsomest apples; sub-acid and pleasant flavor.

Dutchess of Oldenburg. R. D.—Large, striped; tender, juicy, sub-acid; good grower, regular and free bearer. Sept.

Gravenstein.—Very large, striped; tender, rich, sub-acid; profitable. Sept. and Oct.

Lowell, (Rissley.)—Large, waxen yellow; rich and sub-acid; skin oily; vigorous, productive, profitable. Sept. and Oct.

Maiden's Blush. D.—Large, beautiful, yellow with blush cheek; fine quality and prolific. Sept. and Oct.

Pumpkin Sweet.—A very large, yellowish russet; very rich and sweet. Oct. and Nov.

Wolf River. R.—Large, greenish-yellow shaded with crimson; juicy, pleasant, spicy and excellent; tree vigorous and very hardy. Oct. and Nov.

WINTER.

Baldwin.—Large, dark red; sub-acid, good; productive and profitable. Dec. to March.

Ben Davis.—Large, handsome, striped; valuable late keeper. Dec. to March.

Delaware Winter.—New; medium to large; bright red; of fine quality; an early and abundant bearer; vigorous. Keeps until Aug.

Fallawater.—Very large, greenish-yellow with red cheek; good, vigorous and productive. Nov. to March.

Gano.—New; large, deep red and very attractive; tender, mild and sub-acid; a free grower and early bearer; prolific; good shipper and keeper. Feb. to May.

Golden Russet.—Medium, dull russet; crisp juicy, high flavored. Nov. to April.

Grimes' Golden. R.—Large, golden yellow; of best quality; very productive, hardy and vigorous. Jan. to April.

Greening, Rhode I.—Large, green; tender, rich, sub-acid; productive; very popular. Dec. to Apr.

King of T. Co.—A handsome red apple of the largest size and best quality; good grower and bearer. Nov. to March.

Longfield. R.—A medium to large, striped apple; rich, sprightly and sub-acid; free grower and an early and abundant bearer. Dec. to March.

Mann.—Medium to large; yellow; juicy and pleasant; an early and free bearer. Jan. to Apr.

Northern Spy.—Large, striped red; quality excellent; free grower and productive. Dec. to June.

Roxbury Russet.—Medium to large; yellow russet; crisp and good; productive. Jan. to June.

Salome. R.—Medium, striped red and yellow; good quality; withstands wind better than other varieties; bears early and abundantly. Feb. to Aug.

Talman Sweet.—Medium, bright yellow; rich and very sweet; productive. Nov. to Apr.

Twenty Ounce.—A very large, showy, striped apple; brisk and sub-acid; a free grower and very productive; popular.

Walbridge. R—Medium size, handsome, striped; quality good; productive; a good grower and one of the hardiest. March to June.

Wealthy. R.—Medium to large, dark red; sub-acid; a free grower, productive and extra hardy. Dec. to Feb.

CRAB APPLES.

Gen. Grant.—Large and very rich dark red; mild and sub-acid; excellent for dessert; tree a vigorous and upright grower; one of the best. Oct.

Hyslop.—Large, deep crimson; very popular. Oct. to Jan.

Transcendent.—A beautiful variety of the Siberian Crab; red and yellow; very handsome; a remarkable grower and bearer. September and October.

Whitney's No. 20.—One of the largest; green, splashed with carmine; juicy and rich; a great bearer. Aug. and Sept.

PEARS.

See price list on page 29

Pear trees budded onto pear roots are known as Standards. Dwarf pears are budded onto quince roots. Dwarfs come earlier into bearing, usually within two years after planting, but they do not last as long as Standards, unless planted deep so that the point of union between the pear and quince gets several inches under ground, in which case the pear stock will strike roots also, and thus eventually become a Standard. Dwarf pears require more culture, fertilizing and pruning than Standards, but are equally as prolific if, indeed, not more so. All varieties are not equally well adapted for dwarfs and we offer trees of only such as are. Dutchess d'Angouleme and Louise Bonne are most successful on the quince.

Pears are much superior in quality if ripened in the house. Pick them about ten days before they would get ripe on the tree. Winter pears should be left hanging on the trees as long as safe, then pick and store like apples.

Plant Standards about 18 to 20 feet apart each way, and Dwarfs 10 to 12 feet. We can furnish Standard trees of all varieties named, but Dwarfs of only such as have the letter " D " affixed to name.

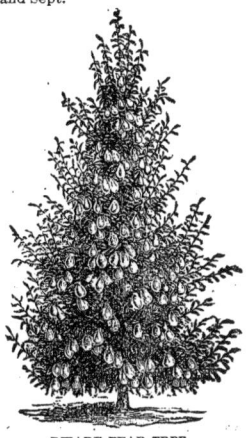

DWARF PEAR TREE.

SUMMER.

Bartlett. D. — Large, yellow; high flavored, juicy, buttery and rich; a vigorous grower and heavy bearer; very popular. Aug. and Sept.

Clapp's Favorite. D.—Much like Bartlett, of which it is a seedling, but larger and a little earlier; very vigorous. Aug.

Osband's Summer. D.—Medium size, yellow with red cheek; mild and pleasant; of fine flavor and productive. Aug.

Lawson or Comet. D.—The largest early pear and exceedingly handsome, though not of high quality; a good shipper and very profitable. Aug.

Le Conte.—Resembles the Kieffer; large, bell shaped; greenish-yellow; handsome; quality second class; a rank grower, early and regular bearer; profitable. Aug.

Tyson. D.—Medium size, yellow and russet; melting, sweet and juicy; vigorous. Aug.

Wilder.—New; the earliest pear and of high quality; medium size; keeps and carries well; very vigorous, hardy and productive. Aug.

AUTUMN.

Buffum.—Medium size, yellow dotted with brown and russet; buttery, rich and sweet; vigorous; one of the best. Sept. and Oct.

Dutchess d'Angouleme. D.—Very large, greenish yellow; juicy, rich and of fine flavor, though rather coarse grained; very popular and profitable. Oct.

Flemish Beauty. D.—Large and beautiful, yellow and russet; juicy, melting, sweet and good; a great bearer; reliable. Sept. and Oct.

Howell.—Large, light yellow with red cheek; handsome, rich, sweet and melting; an early and profuse bearer. Sept. and Oct.

Idaho.—New; very large, nearly round; yellow with brownish red on sunny side; quality best; very hardy, vigorous and prolific. Sept. and Oct.

Kieffer. D.—Large, rich golden with red cheek; very vigorous, healthy and hardy; an early and regular bearer; the best for canning; very profitable. Oct. and Nov.

Louise Bonne. D.—Large, greenish yellow with red cheek; fine quality; a vigorous grower and great bearer. Sept. and Oct.

Seckel. D.—Small, yellowish brown and of the highest flavor and quality; tree a good grower and productive. Sept. and Oct.

Sheldon.—Medium to large; russet red; of best quality; productive. Oct.

WINTER.

Anjou. D.—Very large, greenish yellow; buttery and melting with sprightly, vinous flavor; very vigorous and productive; one of the best and most desirable. Nov. and Dec.

Clairgeau. D.—A very large and handsome market variety; juicy and vinous; bears early and abundantly; profitable. Nov. and Dec.

Easter.—Large, yellow with brown dots; quality good; one of the best winter pears. Dec. to Feb.

Lawrence. D.—Medium to large, yellow with brown dots; melting, pleasant, aromatic. Nov. and Dec.

Mount Vernon. D.—Medium, light russet; juicy and aromatic; early bearer. Nov. and Dec.

QUINCES.

See price list on page 29.

This tree succeeds best in a deep, strong, alluvial soil, though some of the strong growing varieties do well in any good soil. Cultivate, fertilize and prune freely. Plant 10 to 12 feet apart each way.

Angiers.—A vigorous grower and prolific bearer; quality second-class. Oct.

Champion—Larger than Orange, equally as good; more vigorous and productive, but later. Nov. 1st.

Meeche's Prolific.—A very early and regular bearer; wonderfully productive; fruit large,

handsome and of fine quality; one of the best. Oct.

Orange.—Well known and popular; sometimes called the Apple Quince. Oct.

Rea's Mammoth.—A seedling of the Orange; larger, earlier and better; tree very vigorous and productive. Oct.

CHERRIES.

See price list on page 29.

The Heart and Bigarreau cherries are sweet, of larger and more robust growth than Dukes and Morrellos. Plant them 20 feet apart each way. Plant Dukes and Morrellos 15 feet apart. Their growth is slower but much hardier; fruit sour. A dry soil is very essential for cherries.

HEARTS AND BIGARREAUS

Black Tartarian.—Very large, juicy, rich and productive; one of the best. End of June.

Gov. Wood.—Large, light red; juicy, rich and delicious. End of June.

Napoleon Bigarreau.—Very large, pale yellow and red; firm and sweet; profitable, July 1st.

Windsor.—New, large, liver colored; very firm and good; a very late and valuable variety. End of July.

Yellow Spanish.—Large, pale yellow with red cheek; juicy and very good. End of June.

DUKES AND MORRELLOS.

Deyehouse.—New; much like early Richmond, but a week earlier. June.

Early Richmond.—Medium size, red; quite acid; hardy, healthy, very early and productive; the most popular sour cherry. June.

English Morrello.—Large, very dark red; sub-acid, rich and good. End of July.

Louis Phillip.—Medium, rich purplish red; mild sub-acid. July.

May Duke.—Large, dark red; rich, juicy and excellent; popular and reliable. June.

Montmorency. (LARGE.) — Large, light red; tender, sub-acid. One of the best. End of June.

Ostheim.—New Russian; large, dark purplish red; tender, juicy and pleasant; exceedingly hardy; very vigorous and productive.

PLUMS.

See price list on page 29.

Our plums are divided into three classes, viz.: First, The "European," marked by affixing the letter "E" to name; 2nd, The Native American or "Chickasaw," marked by the letter "A," and 3rd, The "Oriental," marked "O." The latter were introduced from China and Japan within the last few years. The American varieties are particularly useful on the Western prairies owing to their great hardiness. Plums do best on a strong, rich soil, containing considerable clay or at least a clay sub-soil. If soil is light, plant trees budded on peach roots, and deep, to avoid the borer.

The most successful plum growers cultivate thoroughly, fertilize and prune annually, and are ever on the watch for the black knot, which is promptly cut off and burned. The curculio is shook off daily into sheets and destroyed (for four weeks from the time the blossoms fall), or else the trees are treated to two or three applications of a very weak solution of Paris green by means of a force pump. The plum is particularly impatient of neglect, but is all the more liberal to the careful and painstaking cultivator. Plant 15 feet apart each way.

Abundance (Botan) O—Very large and early; of a beautiful, bright cherry color. One of the finest and handsomest growers. Very hardy. An early and abundant bearer. Is said to be curculio proof. August.

Bradshaw, E—Very large, purple, juicy, vigorous and productive. August.

Coe's Golden Drop, E—Large, light yellow; firm, rich and sweet; best. End of September.

German Prune, E—Medium, oval, bl . Very

rich and sweet; productive, popular. September.

Guii, E—Very large, blue, sweet and pleasant, though somewhat coarse. Very robust and prolific. September.

Imperial Gage, E—Large, greenish, juicy, rich and desirable. Very vigorous and productive. August.

Lombard, E—Medium, dull brick color, sweet and good. A great bearer and valuable market variety. August.

Marianna, A—A very, rapid grower and remarkably productive. Light red. Medium size. August.

Moore's Arctic, E—Said to be the hardiest plum known. Medium blue, juicy, sweet and pleasant. Very prolific. September.

Niagara, E—Equal to Bradshaw in every respect, except much more productive. August.

Ogan, O—Large, bright golden yellow; firm, sweet, rich and dry. Vigorous and hardy. Early August.

Pottawattamy, A—Large, yellow, vigorous, perfectly hardy and an immense bearer. Early August.

Pond's Seedling, E—Very large and showy, violet red; flesh rather coarse. Very prolific. September.

Reine Claude, E—Very large, greenish, good; productive. September.

Red Egg, E—Large, red, sub-acid; firm and prolific. September.

Shippers' Pride, E—Large, purple, very showy. A free grower; very productive and excellent shipper. Profitable. September.

Shropshire Damson, E—Medium, dark purple. The best of the Damsons. Esteemed for preserving. Curculio proof. October.

Simon's (Prunus Simoni) O—Brick red of an aromatic flavor; better than any Apricot. The tree resembles the peach and is very hardy and productive. August.

SIMONS PLUM.

Washington, E—Very large, green, sweet and good. Very robust and exceedingly productive. One of the best. August.

Weaver, A—Large, purple, good quality; hardy and very prolific. August.

Wild Goose, A—Medium, red, juicy and sweet. July.

Yellow Egg, E—Large, egg shaped. Excellent for cooking. Good and productive. August.

APRICOTS.

See price list on page 30.

The Apricot is one of the most delicious of all fruits. It requires the same kind of soil and treatment as the peach. It is, however, a favorite of the curculio, which must be kept in check as recommended for plums. The Russian varieties (those marked with an "R") are much hardier than the others and peaches, and often succeed where these fail. Plant 15 feet apart each way.

Alexander, R — Large, oblong, yellow and red; sweet and delicious. An immense bearer. One of the best. Early July.

Alexis, R—Very large, yellow, with red cheek. Slightly acid, but rich. A rapid grower and free bearer. Middle July.

Catherine, R—Vigorous and productive, medium size, yellow, mild, sub-acid. End July.

Early Golden—Small, pale orange, juicy and sweet. Productive. July 1st.

Gibb, R—The earliest. Medium size, yellow; fine quality and productive. End of June.

J. L. Budd, R—Large, white and red; juicy,

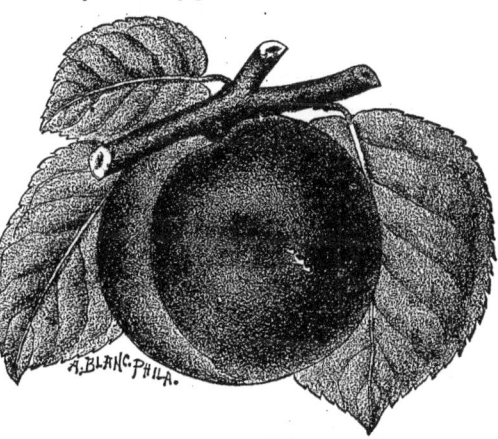

GIBB APRICOT.

sweet and extra fine. The best late variety. Vigorous and prolific. August.

Moorpark—One of the largest. Orange with red cheek. Of a rich flavor and very productive. August.

Nicholas, R—Medium large, white, sweet and melting. Very handsome and valuable. July.

PEACHES.

See price list on page 29.

Peaches succeed best on a warm soil. Keep ground well cultivated and fertilize mostly with wood ashes, lime, &c. Barnyard and other nitrogenous fertilizers produce too rank and soft a growth, thus making them tender. Trim the new growth back annually ⅓ to ½ and part entirely if too dense, before sap starts in spring. Keep out the borer by wrapping the trunk with tarred paper extending some four inches under and as much above the surface of ground. Disease and early death is caused mainly by the borer and starvation. Plant 15 feet apart each way. The white fleshed varieties are marked by affixing the letter "W" to name.

Alexander, W.—Medium; greenish white with red cheek, juicy and sweet. Semi-cling. Aug. 1st.

Crawford's Early—Very large, yellow and red. Best quality; very beautiful and popular; productive; free. Early Sept.

Crawford's Late—Similar to Early Crawford but later and not quite as productive. End Sept.

Beers Smock—Large, yellow with dull red cheek; quality second class, hardy, robust and an immense bearer. Free. Oct.

Early Rivers, W.—Large, creamy white with pink cheek, juicy, sweet and of very rich flavor. Early Aug.

Foster—Much like Early Crawford, but larger and not as prolific. Early Sept.

Chair's Choice—Of largest size, yellow and red, firm; a strong grower and heavy bearer. Free. Sept.

Globe—New. An improved Late Crawford; larger and much more productive; one of the best. Oct. 1st.

Hill's Chili—Medium size, dull yellow; very hardy and a great bearer; free. End Sept.

Mountain Rose, W.—Large, white and carmine, of excellent quality and very reliable. Aug.

Old Mixon Free, W.—Large, white with red cheek; fine quality; very hardy and prolific; reliable. Middle Sept.

Old Mixon Cling, W.—Large, pale yellow and crimson; rich and high flavored; one of the best clingstone peaches. End Sept.

Salway—A very late, large, yellow peach; vigorous; very hardy and productive; free. Middle Oct.

Wager—One of the hardiest, reliable and productive peaches; quality excellent; large, yellow and red; free. End Aug.

Wonderful—New; a very large peach of a rich golden yellow and carmine color; best quality; very vigorous, and productive. Middle Oct.

NECTARINES.

See price list on page 30.

This fruit seems to be a sport of the peach. The only difference consists in its being smooth skinned like a plum. Treat it like the peach.

Boston—Is one of the best ; large, bright yellow with red cheek ; sweet and pleasant. Sept.

NUTS.

See price list on page 30.

Heretofore the culture of nuts has been entirely neglected in this country east of the Rocky Mountains, the supply coming from the forest and importations from Europe. There is, however, no reason why this country should not produce enough to largely export instead of importing them. Aside from the value of the nuts, the timber of some varieties as Walnuts and Hickories is very valuable and becoming more so every year. A word to the wise, etc.

Almond, Hard Shell—Hardy, with large, plump kernel. Very beautiful when in bloom.

Almond, Soft Shell—Not as hardy as the hard shelled, otherwise preferable.

Chestnut, American — Our native variety. Smaller than the Spanish, but sweeter.

Chestnut, Japan—A dwarfish tree, bearing very young. Decidedly ornamental, hardy and productive. The nuts are several times the size of the American and of excellent flavor.

Chestnut, Spanish or Maroon—A hardy tree, producing nuts of very large size and good flavor.

Filbert, English—A shrub growing 6 to 8 feet high, entirely hardy, succeeding on almost all soils, bearing early and abundantly. Larger and better than the native American variety. One of the most profitable and satisfactory nuts to grow.

Hickory, Shell Bark—The best flavored nut. Also a fine shade and valuable timber tree.

Hickory, Pecan—The shell of this variety is much thinner than the Shell Bark, the kernel larger and equally sweet. Found native in the Southern states only, from which fact they were supposed to be tender. Now they are claimed to be hardy at the North also.

Walnut, Black—A lofty, rapid growing native tree. Valuable both for its nuts and timber, which latter is very durable and largely used in the manufacture of furniture and cabinet ware.

Walnut, English or Madeira—This is the large, thin shelled English Walnuts of the fruit stores, of which immense quantities are annually imported. Unlike the native walnuts, the nut drops from its shucks when ripe as readily as those of the hickory. The tree is of lofty growth, very productive, but not fully hardy north of New York city.

Walnut, White or Butternut—A handsome native tree, valuable for shade and timber as well as its nuts.

MULBERRIES.

See price list on page 30.

Downing's Everbearing—Fruit large, black, handsome, sweet and rich ; a rapid grower and productive ; also a fine shade tree.

Russian—A very hardy and rapid growing timber tree. Leaves are used for feeding silk worms. Fruit sweet and good but small.

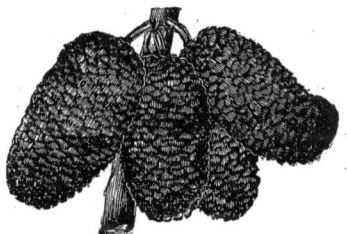

RUSSIAN MULBERRY.

JUNEBERRIES.

See price list on page 30.

The Dwarf Juneberry resembles the swamp huckleberry or whortleberry in appearance and quality but is an entirely different plant. The bush is of the size of the currant, of easiest culture, ironclad hardiness and exceedingly prolific. Very beautiful when covered with its bloom of snowy whiteness. The fruit grows in clusters like currants, of bluish black color ; in flavor mild, rich and sub-acid. Excellent as a desert fruit or canned.

Success—Is the best variety.

FIGS.

See price list on page 30.

The Fig requires protection over winter in the Northern States, which may be given by bending it down and covering it with soil on the approach of severe weather; or the bush may be tied together closely, a loose fitting box put over it and filled in with sawdust; or else they may be planted in tubs and wintered in cellar. They are well worth a little trouble in the way of protection. Plant in warm, dry ground some 6 to 10 feet apart.

Brown Turkey—Brownish purple, large and rich.

Celestial or Sugar—Fruit small but very sweet.

Few people are aware of the commercial value of ornamental trees, vines and shrubs judiciously planted around our homes. Really there is nothing else which, for the amount invested, will produce such grand and valuable results. But because the effect is not immediate many hesitate, delay and even neglect planting, when it would be wisdom to attend to it the first thing.

Plant shade trees along the highway, Maples, Linden, Elm, Horse Chestnut, Catalpa and Mountain Ash are all suitable. In the country, Winter Apples or Cherry trees will also do splendidly. If your buildings are exposed to high winds plant a row or two of Norway Spruce or Austrian Pine on the windward side of them, far enough off to have a roomy yard. It will save you much fuel in winter, to say nothing of the comfort to yourself and domestic animals. Don't make a checker board of your yard or lawn by planting trees and shrubs in regular rows. Mass them in groups or clumps around the edges in such a way as to show them off to best advantage. A Cut Leaf Weeping Birch is always graceful and conspicuous, but especially so against a background of Evergreens or a dark colored building. So are bright flowering shrubs and border plants. Plant shrubs that bloom at different seasons, so as to always have some in flower. A group consisting of shrubs of contrasting colors blooming at the same time and trimmed into a dense clump of oval form cannot fail to please the eyes of every beholder. One of the most graceful and effective clumps I ever saw consisted simply of a few smoke trees allowed to branch from the ground up and trimmed so as to form one mass 16 feet in diameter, standing in full bloom in the middle of a smoothly shaven lawn. Even so simple a thing as a climbing rose, left to grow at its own sweet will, without support, the long brambles drooping down on every side, when in bloom presents a veritable fountain of loveliness. A little taste and effort with a few dollars worth of trees and plants is all that is necessary to make your home appear 50 per cent. richer and brighter. We do not attempt to give but a short description of what we deem the best. For a full list of ornamental trees, etc., we refer you to price list.

DECIDUOUS TREES.

See price list on page 30.

Beech, Rivers Purple-leaved—Very handsome. Foliage crimson in early spring, which changes to a rich, dark purple later in season. For grouping on the lawn with other foliage it cannot be surpassed, but is equally as desirable as a single specimen.

Beech, Fern-leaved—Of elegant round habit, and delicately cut, fern-like foliage.

Birch, Pyramidal—Silvery-white bark with fine pyramidal habit.

Catalpa, Teas Japan—An exceedingly rapid grower with large, luxuriant foliage and spikes of large, handsome white flowers, similar to the Horse Chestnut. Fragrant, entirely hardy.

Cornus, White Flowering Dogwood—A small, native tree producing white flowers 3 to 3½ inches in diameter, early in spring before the leaves begin to appear. Very showy.

Cornus, Red Flowering Dogwood—Similar to the above, except that the flowers are of a deep, rosy pink color.

Elm, Amer. White—The noble, drooping, spreading tree of our forests. One of the grandest park or street trees.

Horse Chestnut, White Flowering—A well known tree of symetrical form, dense habit, dark green foliage, producing large spikes of white flowers abundantly, early in spring.

Horse Chestnut, Double White—Similar to above except having double flowers.

Horse Chestnut, Red Flowering—Very showy, blooms later than the white varieties and does not grow quite as fast.

Laburnum Communis—A small tree with smooth, shining leaves and long drooping racemes of showy, yellow flowers. Very ornamental.

Linden, American—(Basswood)—A rapid growing, beautiful, native tree with large leaves and fragrant flowers, rich in honey.

Linden, Silver-leaved—A handsome, vigorous growing tree with large leaves, whitish on underside, which produce a beautiful appearance when stirred by the wind. One of the best.

Magnolia, Acuminata—(Cucumber Tree)—A beautiful native tree with rich large leaves and fragrant flowers.

Magnolia Soulangeana—Flowers white and purple. One of the finest and handsomest.

Magnolia Speciosa—Flowers a little smaller, lighter and fully a week later than Soulangeana.

Maple, Wier's Cut-leaved—A silver Maple with remarkable and beautiful dissected foliage. A

rapid grower; shoots, slender and drooping, giving it a very graceful appearance.

Maple, Norway—A distinct, foreign variety with large, broad leaves of a deep, rich green color. The most desirable for street, park or lawn.

Maple, Schwedlerii—A purple-leaved variety of the Norway Maple. The young shoots and leaves are of a very bright crimson color, changing to a purplish green in the older leaves. Very valuable.

Mountain Ash, European—A fine hardy tree; head dense and regular. Covered in June with a mass of white flowers, later with yellow berries, which turn into bright scarlet and last long into the winter. Very beautiful.

Salisburia—(Maiden Hair Tree)—A singular cone-bearing, deciduous tree with peculiar leaves. Beautiful.

Thorn—(Hawthorn)—A small tree of somewhat irregular growth. Exceedingly beautiful when in bloom during June, densely loaded with large clusters of flowers resembling double daisies. We have them in three colors, double white, double scarlet and Paul's new double or crimson.

WEEPING DECIDUOUS TREES.

See price list on page 31.

Mt. Ash, European Weeping—An awkward, straggling tree. Very conspicuous.

Beech Weeping—A remarkably peculiar tree. Quite vigorous, growing to the height of 30 feet or over. Of wonderful grace and beauty when covered with its rich and luxuriant foliage.

Birch, Cut-leaf Weeping—Deservedly one of the most popular of all weeping trees. A strong, upright grower with graceful drooping branches. Silvery white bark and delicately cut foliage.

Elm, Camperdown—A vigorous weeping tree sufficient in itself to make a good-sized arbor, roof and all.

Mulberry, Teas Weeping—A graceful, beautiful, weeping tree forming a perfect umbrella-shaped head, with long, slender, willowy branches drooping to the ground and gracefully swaying in the wind. Foliage small, lobed, and of a delightfully fresh, glossy green. A rapid grower and exceedingly hardy.

Willow, Babylon—Our common well known weeping willow.

Willow, Kilmarnock—One of the most beautiful of the low growing, weeping varieties. Vigorous grower and quite distinct in appearance.

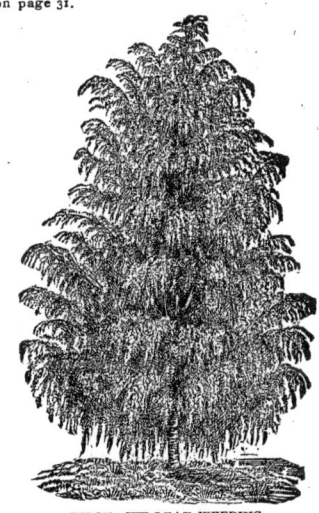

BIRCH, CUT-LEAF WEEPING.

DECIDUOUS SHRUBS.

See price list on page 31.

Althea, or Rose of Sharon—This beautiful shrub flowers late in summer when most others are out of bloom. It bears large double flowers similar to the hollyhock very abundantly on strong, erect branches. Very hardy and of easiest cultivation. White, red, purple and striped; all double.

Althea, Variegated—Leaves bright green, broadly margined with light yellow; very showy.

Almond—A beautiful small shrub blooming early in June; branches are literally covered with flowers of size and shape of daisies; double white and double pink.

Berberry, Common European—A spiny shrub, blooming in May and June, with drooping racemes of yellow flowers followed by bright orange-scarlet berries.

Berberry, Purple Leaved—Same as above except in foliage, which is a rich violet-purple all summer.

Calycanthus, Sweet Scented Shrub—An interesting shrub having a rare and peculiar fragrance of wood and flowers. It blooms abundantly in June and at intervals through the summer.

CORNUS E. VARIAGATA.

Cornus, Elegantisima, Var.—(Variegated Dogwood.)—One of the handsomest variegated leaved shrubs. Bark brilliant red, leaves green, broadly margined with white.

Deutzia, Gracilis—A charming variety and very hardy. An abundant bloomer of pure white flowers about Decoration Day, on which account it is very popular.

Deutzia, Crenata—Similar to above but flowers are double white and tinged with rose.

Exochordia, Grandiflora—A fine shrub producing large white flowers profusely in May.

Forsythia, or Golden Bell—A hardy shrub blooming freely early in spring.

Hydrangea, Grandiflora—One of the most popular of hardy shrubs. It has large, rich, abundant foliage, immense pyramidal shaped panicles of white flowers, changing to pink in August and continuing until frost. Fertilize well and prune severely.

Prunus Pissardii, Purple Leaved Plum—Foliage of a bright purplish red, remaining so all through the season. Entirely hardy; one of the most valuable hardy foliage shrubs on the list.

Prunus Triloba—(Double Flowering Plum.)—Blooms much like flowering Almond, but earlier and larger, of a delicate pink color. Hardy and exceedingly handsome.

Purple Fringe, Smoke Tree—A shrub or small tree of spreading habit, covered in mid-summer with a profusion of dusky hair-like flowers. Strikingly peculiar and beautiful.

Quince, Japan—An old and esteemed shrub bearing a profusion of bright scarlet flowers in early spring. Makes a lovely hedge.

Philadelphus, (Syringa or Mock Orange,) Golden Leaved—Dwarf and very compact. The foliage is dense and of a golden yellow throughout the season. Hardy and useful for grouping with other foliage shrubs, especially those of a dark color.

Double Syringa—A double flowering variety of the popular Mock Orange. Fragrant and as double as a rose. Very choice and desirable.

Wiegela—Shrubs of erect habit while young, but gradually spread and droop as they grow older. In June and July they produce masses of superb large trumpet shaped flowers of all shades, from pure white to red. Very effective; eight varieties.

SPIREA.

These are all low shrubs of easy culture and blooming extends over a period of three months.

Billardi—Rose color; blooms nearly all summer.

Collosa Alba—A white flowering variety of dwarf habit.

Plum Leaved, Double Flowering—Very beautiful; blooms in May. Its flowers are like white daisies.

Douglas—Has spikes of lovely deep rose colored flowers in July and August.

Lance Leaved—Narrow, pointed leaves and large, round clusters of white flowers that cover the whole plant. Blooms in May; charming.

Reeve's Double—Flowers white and double. Blooms freely in clusters. One of the best.

Van Houttei—One of the most charming and beautiful of the Spireas. Plant remarkably vigorous, hardy and profuse bloomer. Flowers are pure white and produced in great clusters.

CLIMBING PLANTS.

See price list on page 31.

Ampelopsis, Veitchii—(Japan Ivy). One of the finest of ornamental climbers. It clings firmly to stone, brick or wood and is entirely hardy. Foliage small but rich and dense, changing in autumn to carmine and gold of exceeding brilliancy.

Clematis, Jackmanii—The flowers when fully expanded are from four to six inches in diameter. Rich purple, with a velvety appearance. It blooms profusely and continually from July until frost.

Clematis, Henrii—This variety has even larger and more perfect blossoms than the Jackmanii and is white as snow, but is not quite as prolific.

Wistaria, Chinese Blue—A most beautiful climber of rapid growth, producing large, pendulous clusters of pale blue flowers in May.

Wistaria, Chinese White—Much like the above, except the flowers are white and last longer.

Wistaria, Double Purple — A strong, free climber and entirely hardy. The flowers are perfectly double on racemes of remarkable length.

EVERGREENS.

See price list on page 32.

Arbor Vitæ (American)—Well known. A rapid grower. Very desirable for hedges.

Arbor Vitæ, Siberian—Of rather slow growth, very compact and symmetrical and of a pretty dark green color. Exceedingly hardy.

Arbor Vitæ, Tom Thumb—Of dwarf habit, hardy and valuable for small grounds.

Juniper, Irish—A popular variety. Very erect, forming a column of deep green foliage. Useful in small places and for contrast.

Juniper, Virginia—The red cedar. A well known native tree. Makes a fine ornamental hedge.

Pine, Austrian—A remarkably robust, hardy, spreading tree; leaves long, stiff and dark green. A rapid grower.

Pine, Montana or Dwarf—A low, curious, spreading specie, attaining only the size of a bush.

Pine, Scotch—A well known, robust, rapid growing tree of dull bluish green foliage.

Spruce, Colorado Blue—The choicest and most beautiful of all evergreens. Of compact growth, symmetrical, pyramidal form with foliage of a rich steel blue color. Very hardy.

Spruce, Hemlock or Weeping—An elegant pyramidal tree

C. BLUE SPRUCE.

with drooping branches and delicate dark foliage. A lovely lawn tree, also makes a highly ornamental hedge.

Spruce, Norway—A valuable tree either as single specimen or for grouping; also makes a fine hedge. Very popular.

ROSES.

See price list on page 32.

HYBRID PERPETUALS.

The following are all hardy, and yet a slight protection in exposed situations is desirable. They all bloom profusely in June and more or ess through the summer. Fertilize and prun freely.

Alfred Colomb—Very large and full. Brillian carmine crimson; extremely fragrant. A fre grower.

Annie De Diesbach—Very large, Brilliant crimson; fragrant, vigorous.

Baron De Bonstetten.—Flowers large and very double; color rich, dark red, passing to deep velvety maroon. Very fragrant.

Caroline De Sansal—Pale flesh color, large and full. Vigorous.

Coquette Des Alps—White, slightly shaded with carmine. Vigorous and free bloomer.

Coquette Des Blanches—Pure white, of medium size, but full and very pretty. A free grower.

Gen. Jacqueminot—Brilliant velvety crimson, large and showy. A free grower and bloomer.

Gen. Washington—Large, flat, brilliant rosy crimson; prolific. A moderate grower.

John Hopper—Bright rose, with carmine center. Large and full, very fragrant. Free grower.

La France—Rich satiny peach, changing to deep rose; large and full. A constant bloomer. The sweetest of all. Free grower.

Louis Van Houtte—Bright crimson, large, full and fragrant. Moderate grower.

Mrs. Laing—Very free flowering; commences early and continues to bloom profusely until fall. Of delicate pink color. Very fragrant

Mad. Plantier—Pure white, large and very double. A free bloomer and grower.

Magna Charta—Pink and carmine; very large and full; a profuse bloomer. Fragrant. Free grower.

Marshall P. Wilder—Bright cherry carmine; very fragrant and one of the freest bloomers. Vigorous.

Madam Masson—Large and double, redish crimson. A constant bloomer.

Paul Neyron—The largest of all. Deep rose color. A free bloomer and vigorous grower.

Prince C. De Rohan—Deep velvety crimson; large, moderately full. Free grower.

Persian Yellow—Deep golden yellow. The finest hardy yellow rose grown.

MOSS ROSES.

Admired for the curious mossy covering of the buds. The following are all free growers, perfectly hardy and the best of this class:

Capt. Jno. Ingraham—Dark velvety purple; full and fine.

Comptesse De Murinais—White, tinged with flesh. Large.

Glory of Mosses—Pale rose, very large, full and beautiful.

Perpetual White—Pure white; blossoms in clusters.

Princess Adelaide—Blush, becoming quite pale. Very double.

CLIMBING ROSES.

These are particularly useful for training over arbors, verandas, pillars, etc., and for covering unsightly objects. All are rank growers and perfectly hardy.

Baltimore Belle—Pale blush, nearly white. Blooms in clusters.

Gem of the Prairie—Bright crimson, large and double. Fragrant.

Seven Sisters—Crimson, changing gradually to white.

Prairie Queen—Bright rosy red. Very large and fine.

Boquet of Choice New Fruit

Grapes.

Brilliant.—Red. Described as very vigorous, hardy, healthy, and productive. Equal in size to the Concord in bunch and berry, but having tougher skin, carries better. Very handsome, equal to the Delaware in quality and ripens several days earlier. Not yet tested by us.

Colerain.—New white. Bunch medium to large, berries medium, very sweet, tender and of excellent quality. It ripens with Moore's Early, but will keep until frost without dropping its berries. A vigorous grower, abundant bearer and perfectly hardy and healthy.

Currants.

Black Champion.—New. The best black currant of European origin. Very large in bunch and of excellent quality. A very strong, robust grower.

North Star.—New. A chance seedling from Minn. It is an exceedingly vigorous grower. Canes often grow to a length of 3 to 4 feet in one season. It is extremely hardy, productive, and very mild in flavor. While the individual berries do not grow quite as large as the Cherry Currant, its bunches are very large, averaging 4 inches long. Very desirable and profitable.

Blackberries.

El Dorado.—New. A chance seedling found in Ohio some 13 years ago, which, in all that time never failed to produce a full crop except once, when a late May frost killed all blackberry blossoms. It is described as of good size, extreme hardiness, great productiveness, and extra fine quality. A strong grower and healthy. Very promising.

Red Raspberries.

Loudon.—New. Originated by F. W. Loudon of Wis. and claimed to be similar to Cuthbert but larger, firmer and much more productive. Not yet tested by us. E. S. Carman, editor of the Rural New Yorker, than whom there is no better authority in the U. S., says: "The Loudon is the best hardy late red raspberry we have ever tried, ripening with the Cuthbert; averages larger. Very firm, continuing later, and among the heaviest yielders I have tried."

Royal Church.—New. Has been thoroughly tested at most of the agricultural experiment stations of the country, and not one unfavorable report has been made. It is aromatic, sprightly and delicious, excellent for table and preserves. It is a vigorous grower and perfectly hardy. Over 150 berries have been counted on a single stem, averaging over ¾ inch in diameter. Earlier than Cuthbert and continues longer in bearing.

Strawberries.

Enhance.—New. One of the very best market varieties. Exceedingly vigorous, healthy and productive. Very firm and of a bright crimson color. Large and uniform in size. One of the best for fertilizing pistillate varieties.

Greenville, P—It has been tried thoroughly at the experimental stations for the past five years, and reports are unanimous in its favor. It leads for productiveness, market, home-use and general purpose; combines earliness, firmness, large size, good quality, very even and fine color, with wonderful vigor and health of plant.

Splendid.—Probably the best general purpose strawberry before the public today. A strong, healthy grower, prolific as Warfield, nearly as large as Bubach, perfect flowering, uniform in size and shape. Very firm, brilliant color, and one of the best in quality.

Timbrell, P.—New. Robust in growth, with rank, dark green foliage, and very productive. The berries are large, even and of a dark crimson color throughout. Very handsome and so firm it will stand long shipments in good condition. The latest to bloom and ripen.

Van Deman.—The most promising extra early market berry. Has been tested at all the experimental stations, where it is highly recommended. Of good fair size, brilliant color, very firm, even shape, and high flavor. The plant is a strong grower, healthy, robust, and productive.

Peaches.

Crosby.—The constant and abundant bearing, often when all others failed, has brought this variety into public favor. It is the hardiest peach known. The tree grows low and spreading. Fruit is of medium size, bright orange yellow splashed with carmine, and ripens with Old Mixon Free. It has become very popular.

Photo-Engraving of fair samples of Our goods, reduced to 1-18 nat length and diameter.

1.	Dwarf Pear	2 to 3 feet.
2.	" "	3 to 4 feet.
3.	Standard Pear	3 to 4 feet.
4.	" "	4 to 5 feet.
5.	" "	5 to 7 feet.
6.	Duke and Morrello Cherries	4 to 5 feet.
7.	" "	3 to 4 feet.
8.	Peach Tree	4 to 5 feet.
9.	" "	3 to 4 feet.
10.	" "	2 to 3 feet.
11.	Asparagus Roots	1 year.
12.	" "	2 year.
13.	Grape Vine	2 year, No. 1.
14.	Grape Vine	1 y
15.	" "	1 y
16.	Currant Plant	1 ye
17.	" "	1 ye
18.	" "	2 ye
19.	Gooseberry Plant	1 ye
20.	" "	1 ye
21.	" "	2 ye
22.	Blackberry root cutting plant.	
23.	" sucker plant.	
24.	Black Raspberry plant.	
25.	Red Raspberry plant.	

The Standard Pear trees also fairly represent our Apple, Plum and Heart & Bigarrea trees as to size and quality. Note the abundance of fibrous roots.

To Our Friends and Patrons.

Grape Vines our Specialty.—For twelve years have we made the propagation of grape vines our great specialty, increasing our planting largely and steadily every year. The more we grow the more we sell; and the more we sell the further our reputation for superior stock gets spread. Every satisfactory vine, plant or tree sent out is a salesman, a perpetual advertisement, and a monument to our success. Our superiority in this line is mainly owing to a peculiarity of our soil and climate in which we can raise *strong and fibrous rooted vines* quickly. In fact, we raise as large vines in one season here as are usually grown in two elsewhere, and of much superior quality. Many nurserymen prefer to buy what vines they sell of us rather than propagate them themselves. This, in part, accounts for the rapid and enormous growth of our busine s. But while we make Grape Vines our specialty, we also produce large quantities of other stock. 1st, Because we can raise equally well, superior rooted currants, gooseberries, and other stock; and, 2nd, Because the grape vine trade naturally brings along with it orders for trees, plants, etc.

Our Facilities.— For our convenience and that of our customers we have built a frost-proof cellar 60x100 feet and 9½ feet high in which we store, over winter, all our grape vines, currants, gooseberries, blackberries, red raspberries and a part of our trees and ornamentals. Attached to the cellar is the packing house, 30x40 feet. This room as well as the cellar and yard are amply provided with water by the Fredonia Water Works. Attached to the packing house are rooms for the storage of packing cases, moss, straw, labels, etc., also the grading room, which is connected with the office by an underground speaking-tube. Into this room, heated by a stove, the grape vines, currants, etc., are brought during the winter, a wheel-barrow load at a time, and carefully graded into the various sizes as 2 yr., No. 1; 1 yr., No. 1; 1 yr., No. 2, and culls. The culls we do not offer for sale. The several grades are tied up neatly into bunches of 100 each, except the 2 yr., No. 1, which are tied in bunches of 50. Then they are promptly put back into the cellar and another load brought in. By this means we get leisure to do the grading very carefully, we know to a plant what we have to sell, and have the stock in readiness for packing in the spring. Thus we are enabled to do a much larger business more satisfactory to our customers as well as ourselves, than would be possible were we obliged to do the digging and grading in spring in addition to the packing and planting. Moreover, it facilitates the filling of orders to the South and Pacific States during the winter and before the ground thaws here to admit of digging. From a personal experience of eight years we know that nursery stock is much safer in the cellar than in the open ground where it is exposed to wind, wet, and often intense cold. We have never stored any in cellar that did not come out as fresh and bright in spring as it went in in the fall.

Cold Storage.—Having our stock in cellar where we have perfect control over the temperature, we have no trouble in keeping it dormant and in excellent shipping order until May 20th, and longer were it necessary, thus extending the planting season several weeks. However, parties ordering late in the season should mention a second choice as stock of first choice may be exhausted.

No Orders Refused.—It does not pay to put up orders of less amount than $1, and most nurserymen refuse to accept such. We, however, agree to carefully fill each and every order, no matter how small, so long as our stock lasts, being confident that our goods will please and bring further trade that does pay. In order to better introduce our goods, we offer to mail for fourteen cents, two one year No. 1 vines as samples, (*one kind only, of our selection*) to show size and quality of our vines.

Superior Packing.—Our packing, for which we charge nothing, is not excelled by any other establishment. Not only do we pack with a view to entire safety, but also as lightly as possible, in order to reduce transportation charges to a minimum. We pack our goods to carry safely to any part of the world. Everything is carefully labeled. Strawberries are packed in crates with plenty of ventilation to avoid heating.

Transportation Charges.—Inquiries about cost of shipping usually come during the packing season when we are busiest, so that we are not always able to give them the attention we would like to. But you can find out for yourself by inquiring of your express or freight agent. The rate from this place is often less than the rate to this place and by estimating the weight of the goods when packed an approximate amount may be arrived at. The weight of our stock when packed to go by mail is about as follows per 100; Grape Vines, Currants and Gooseberries, 2 yr., No. 1, 20 lbs ; 1 yr., No. 1, 12½ lbs.; 1 yr., No. 2, 8 lbs.; Blackberries, 7 lbs.; Raspberries, 5 lbs.; Strawberries, 2½ lbs.; Asparagus, 2 yr., 6 lbs.; 1 yr., 4 lbs. Fruit and Ornamental Trees not packed, 5 to 7 ft., 125 lbs.; 4 to 5 ft., 80 lbs. Smaller trees and shrubs in proportion. Packed to go by express they weigh about one-half more and by freight twice as much.

Order Early.—Make your plans and order stock before the hurry of spring is upon you, and while you have leisure. Their are many advantages to be gained by this. Always name the date when you want stock sent.

Our Guarantee.—We warrant all our stock true to name and of quality represented to this extent that should any prove otherwise we hereby agree, upon proper proof, to refund the money received for the same, or else replace with others that are true. But we are not liable for damages other than herein named.

Our References.—Regarding our reliability and responsibility we would refer you to the Fredonia National Bank, Miner's Bank, Postmaster, Express Agent, or any other public man or institution here. When inquiring do not forget to enclose a self-directed and stamped envelope for reply Your own banker may also be able to give you our standing from the Mercantile Reports.

HORTICULTURAL PUBLICATIONS.

As many of our customers wish further information on growing Fruit and Ornamentals than is possible to give in a catalogue, we have made arrangements by which we can furnish the following at publishers' own prices. We heartily recommend them as the best obtainable on the subjects treated. Sent postpaid on receipt of price.

Our Native Grape.—By Chas. Mitzky. The best and newest work on Grape Culture in all its bearings, brought right up to date. Its History, Propagation, Hybridizing, Grafting, Selection of Location, Soil, Fertilizers, Trellises, Pruning, Training, Packing and Packages, Insects and Diseases, with their remedies and preventatives. Descriptions of nearly 900 varieties, etc., are all exhaustively treated by a scientific, experienced and practical grape grower, assisted by the best authorities of this country. Neither amateur nor vineyardist can afford to get along without this book. 250 pages, fully illustrated. Price, in paper cover, $1 00; cloth. $1.50.

Fuller's Small Fruit Culturist.—The most valuable work on the subject extant. Propagation, culture, varieties, etc., fully treated upon. Profusely illustrated. Price, $1.50.

Barry's Fruit Garden.—Treats of the Nursery, Fruit Garden and Orchard in all its branches; soils, manure, culture,pruning, varieties, etc. New and revised edition, fully illustrated; 500 pages. Price, $2.00.

Fungus Diseases of the Grape, Etc—By F. Lamson-Scribner, Prof. of Botany, University of Tenn. This book gives a full description of each disease, its nature, means of identification, with remedies to be used, and modes of application. Copiously illustrated. Price, in paper cover, 50 cents; cloth, 75 cents.

Horticulturist' Rule Book.—Contains, in handy and concise form, a great number of rules and receipts required by fruit growers, gardeners, florists, farmers, etc. Compiled by L. H. Bailey, Prof. of Horticulture in Cornell University. Invaluable. Price, in cloth, 50 cents.

Horticultural Art Folio.—A book of 50 colored plates of the best and most popular varieties of fruits and flowers, executed in the highest style of the lithographer's art, bound in flexible clot covers, together with an 80 page illustrated, descriptive catologue. Splendid for soliciting orders for vines, plants and trees. Price, $2.00.

Landscape Gardening,—By Elias A. Long. A new, practical treatise on Landscape Gardening, just published. It comprises 32 diagrams of actual grounds with copious explanations. It contains the best information on the subject right up to date. Beautifully illustrated and printed on heavy plate paper. Price, 50 cents.

Farm Journal.—Published monthly at Philadelphia, Pa. Instructive, reliable, progressive. The cream of farm periodicals. 50 cents a year, but free with order for nursery stock of $1.00 or more at single rates, if mentioned in order.

TERMS AND PRICE LIST.

SPRING, 1895.

Five, fifty and four hundred of a kind at ten, hundred and thousand rates, respectively. 100 and 1,000 of a class, as grapes, raspberries, etc., if not to exceed five varieties at 100 or 1,000 rates, respectively. $20.00 worth or over at lowest rate named. Of grape vines and small fruits $5.00 worth at 100 rates.

Transportation.—All stock will be shipped by express or freight as desired, at purchaser's expense, except as follows: Grape vines, small fruits and small plants of ornamentals will be sent by mail postpaid, at single and ten rates. Small trees, cut back, of all fruit and many ornamental trees may also be mailed at ½ the single rates of largest size priced. If 50 or more are desired at 100 rates, postage must be added according to the following table.

POSTAGE	PER 50	PER 100	POSTAGE	PER 50	PER 100,
Grapes, Currants and Gooseberries, 2 year No. 1	$0 80	$1 50	Blackberries	$0 30	$0 50
The same, 1 year No 1	55	1 00	Strawberries	15	25
Raspberries	25	40	Asparagus, 2 years	30	50
			Asparagus, 1 year	20	35

Our vines and plants are very strong, hence the large amount of postage required. The postage on No. 2 grape vines, currants and gooseberries is but ⅔ as much as on No. 1.

Club Orders.—Parties requiring but few vines and plants are invited to take advantage of our offer to send $5.00 worth of Grape Vines and Small Fruits at 100 rates or $20.00 worth of anything on this list at lowest rates named, by clubbing in with or taking orders of their neighbors.

Early Orders will be booked if accompanied by at least one-quarter of amount. The balance may be sent with order to ship.

Substituting—In case we are out of a variety or size called for we reserve the right to substitute another similar variety of equal merit or another size or grade to an equal value, unless the words "No Substituting" are written on the order, in which case we will fill the order as far as we can and return the balance.

Larger and Smaller Vines. Plants and trees than those named will be furnished as follows: 3 year No. 1 grape vines, currants and gooseberries at ¼ additional to price of 2 year No. 1; 1 year No. 2, at ⅔ the price of 1 year No. 1; ¼ Larger trees and shrubs at ¼ larger price; double the size for double the price; ½ the size for ⅔ the price; ⅔ the size for ¾ the price.

Claims for Errors, if any, must be made within 5 days after receipt of goods. Those made after a lapse of 10 days will not be entertained.

Terms—Cash with order. Remit by postal or express order, bank draft or registered letter, at our risk. Money loose in ordinary letters is at the risk of the sender. Individual checks for less than $50.00 must be made out for 25 cents extra to cover exchange. $5.00 worth or more sent C. O. D. if desired, provided at least one-quarter of the amount accompanies the order. Return charges on the money will be added in all cases.

FRUIT DEPARTMENT.

For "A Bouquet of New Fruits" see page 24.

GRAPE VINES.

By Mail, Post-paid at Single and Ten Rates,	1 Year, No. 1			2 Years, No. 1.		
	each	10	100	each	10	100
Agawam (Rog. 15)	$0 10	$0 80	$3 00	$0 12	$1 00	$4 00
Amber	18	1 50	6 00	30	2 50	9 00
Amber Queen....	20	1 70	7 00	30	2 50	9 00
Aminia (Rog. 39)..	12	1 00	4 00	18	1 50	6 00
August Giant....	20	1 70	7 00	30	2 50	10 00
Bacchus	10	80	3 00	12	1 00	4 00
Barry (Rog. 43)...	35	2 75	11 00	50	4 00	16 00
Berkmans	45	3 50	15 00	65	5 50	25 00
Black Eagle	30	2 50	10 00	45	3 75	15 00
Brighton	12	1 00	4 00	20	1 70	7 00
Brilliant, new....	1 25	10 00		1 75	15 00	
Catawba	10	80	2 50	12	1 00	4 00
Centennial	40	3 30	14 00	60	5 00	23 00
Champion	10	80	2 50	12	1 00	3 50
Clinton	10	80	2 50	12	1 00	3 50
Colerain	75	6 00		1 00	9 00	
Concord	10	80	2 00	12	1 00	3 00
Concord Muscat...	75	6 00	30 00	1 25	10 00	50 00
Cottage	10	80	3 00	12	1 00	4 00
Cynthiana	20	1 70	7 00	30	2 50	10 00
Delaware	18	1 50	6 00	25	2 00	8 00
Diana	12	1 00	3 50	15	1 25	5 00
Dracut Amber...	12	1 00	4 00	18	1 50	6 00
Duchess	12	1 00	4 00	18	1 50	5 50
Early Ohio	1 00	7 50	50 00	1 50	12 00	75 00
Early Victor....	12	1 00	4 00	18	1 25	6 00
Eaton	25	2 00	8 00	35	3 00	12 00
El Dorado	40	3 00	13 00	60	5 00	18 00
Elvira	10	80	2 50	12	1 00	3 50
Empire State....	15	1 25	5 00	22	1 80	7 00
Essex (Rog. 41)...	25	2 00	8 00	35	3 00	12 00
Etta	15	1 25	5 00	22	1 80	7 00
Eumelan..	30	2 50	11 00	45	4 00	15 00
Gaertner (Rog. 14)	30	2 50	10 00	45	3 75	15 00
Geneva, new....	35	3 00	12 00	50	4 25	18 00
Goethe (Rog. 1)...	18	1 50	6 00	25	2 00	8 00
Green Mountain..	60	5 00	25 00	90	7 50	40 00
Grein's Golden...	15	1 25	5 00	25	2 00	7 00
Hartford	10	80	3 00	12	1 00	4 00
Hayes	18	1 50	6 00	25	2 00	8 00
Herbert (Rog. 44).	18	1 50	6 00	25	2 00	8 00
Highland	50	4 00	18 00	75	6 00	30 00
Iona	10	80	3 00	15	1 25	5 00
Isabella	10	80	2 50	12	1 00	3 50
Ives	10	80	2 50	12	1 00	3 50
Janesville	18	1 50	6 00	25	2 00	8 00
Jewell, new....	75	6 00	30 00	1 00	7 50	40 00
Jefferson	25	2 00	9 00	40	3 00	14 00
Jessica	30	2 50	10 00	45	4 00	14 00
Lady	15	1 25	5 00	22	1 80	7 00
Lady Washington	45	4 00	15 00	75	6 00	26 00
Leader, new....	45	4 00	15 00	75	6 00	24 00
Lindley (Rog, 9)..	10	80	2 50	12	1 00	3 50
Martha	10	80	3 00	12	1 00	4 00

By Mail, Post-paid at Single and Ten Rates.	1 Year, No. 1.			2 Years, No. 1.		
	each	10	100	each	10	100
Massasoit (Rog. 3)	$0 15	$1 25	$5 00	$0 22	$1 80	$7 00
Maxatawney....	20	1 65	7 00	30	2 50	9 00
Merrimac(Rog. 19)	12	1 00	4 00	18	1 50	6 00
Montefiore	18	1 50	6 00	27	2 25	9 00
Mo. Reissling....	12	1 00	4 00	18	1 50	6 00
Moore's Diamond.	18	1 50	6 00	30	2 50	9 00
Moore's Early...	15	1 25	5 00	22	1 80	7 00
Moyer	25	2 00	8 00	40	3 00	14 00
Mills, new	75	6 00	30 00	1 00	9 00	40 00
Nectar, new....	80	7 00	30 00	1 20	10 00	40 00
Niagara	10	80	3 00	12	1 00	4 00
Noah	10	80	3 00	12	1 00	4 00
Norton's Va....	20	1 50	7 00	30	2 25	10 00
Norwood.	50	4 00	20 00	75	6 00	30 00
Oneida	35	3 00	12 00	50	4 00	17 00
Perkins	15	1 25	5 00	22	1 80	7 00
Pocklington	18	1 50	6 00	30	2 50	9 00
Poughkeepsie....	50	4 00	20 00	75	6 00	30 00
Prentiss	18	1 50	6 00	25	2 00	8 00
Rebecca	30	2 50	12 00	45	3 75	18 00
Requa (Rog. 28)...	25	2 00	8 00	35	3 00	12 00
Rochester	1 00	8 00	50 00	1 50	12 00	75 00
Salem |R 22 or 53].	10	80	3 00	15	1 25	5 00
Telegraph	12	1 00	4 00	18	1 50	6 00
Triumph	75	6 00	30 00	1 25	10 00	50 00
Ulster Prolific...	22	1 80	7 00	35	3 00	11 00
Vergennes	12	1 00	4 00	18	1 50	6 00
Victoria	50	4 00	20 00	75	6 00	30 00
Wilder (Rog. 4)...	12	1 00	4 00	18	1 50	6 00
Woodruff Red...	30	2 50	11 00	50	4 00	16 00
Worden	10	80	2 50	12	1 00	3 50
Wyoming Red...	12	1 00	4 00	18	1 50	6 00

Currants.

	each	10	100	each	10	100
Black Champion..	15	1 20	5 00	20	1 50	7 00
Cherry	12	1 00	3 50	18	1 50	5 00
Crandall	25	2 00	8 00	35	3 00	12 00
Fay's Prolific....	12	1 00	5 00	20	1 50	7 00
La Versailles....	12	1 00	3 50	18	1 50	5 00
Lee's Prolific....	12	1 00	3 50	18	1 50	5 00
North Star....	40	3 30	14 00	60	5 00	23 00
Red Dutch	12	1 00	3 50	18	1 50	5 00
Victoria	12	1 00	3 50	18	1 50	5 00
White Grape....	12	1 00	3 50	18	1 50	5 00

Gooseberries.

	each	10	100	each	10	100
Chautauqua.	1 00	8 50		1 50	12 50	
Downing	18	1 50	6 00	25	2 00	8 00
Houghton	12	1 00	4 00	18	1 50	6 00
Industry	35	3 00	12 00	50	4 00	16 00
Smith's Improved.	20	1 65	7 00	30	2 50	10 00

By Mail, Post-paid, at Ten Rates.	Per 10	Per 100	Per 1000
Raspberries.			
Cuthbert, red	$0 40	$1 25	$10 00
Doolittle, black	40	1 25	10 00
Golden Queen, yellow	60	2 00	15 00
Gregg, black	40	1 25	10 00
Johnston's Sweet, black	50	1 50	12 00
Kansas, new, black	90	3 00	25 00
Loudon, new, red, each 60c	5 00		
Marlboro, red	40	1 25	10 00
Ohio, black	40	1 25	10 00
Palmer, new, black	50	1 50	12 00
Philadelphia, red	40	1 25	10 00
Royal Church, new, red	1 50	5 00	
Shaeffers Col., purple	50	1 50	12 00
Sonhegan, black	40	1 25	10 00
Thompson's Early Prolific	50	1 50	12 00
Blackberries			
Ancient Briton	75	2 50	20 00
Early Harvest	60	2 00	15 00
El Dorado, new, each 40c	3 00	15 00	
Erie, new	90	3 00	25 00
Kittatinny	60	2 00	15 00
Lucretia Dewberry	60	2 00	15 00
Minnewaski, new	90	3 00	25 00
Snyder	50	1 50	12 00
Stone's Hardy	60	2 00	15 00
Taylor's Prolific	60	2 00	15 00
Wachussetts Thornless	75	2 50	20 00
Wilson's Early	60	2 00	15 00
Wilson, Jr.	60	2 00	15 00
Strawberries.			
Bidwell	25	50	3 50
Bubach's No. 5, P	30	60	4 00
Chas. Downing	30	60	4 00
Crawford	30	60	4 00
Crescent Seedling, P	25	50	3 00
Cumberland Triumph	30	60	4 00
Enhance, new	35	75	6 00
Gandy	30	60	4 00
Greenville, P., new	35	75	6 00
Haverland, P	30	60	4 00
James Vick	25	50	3 50
Jessie	25	50	3 50
Kentucky	30	60	4 00
Manchester	30	60	4 00
Michel's Early	25	50	3 00
Miner's Prolific	30	60	4 00
Sharpless	25	50	3 50
Splendid, new	1 00	2 50	20 00
Timbrell, P., new	1 00	2 50	20 00
Van Deman, new	35	75	6 00
Warfield, P	25	50	3 50
Wilson's Albany	25	50	3 00
Garden Roots.			
Asparagus—Conover's Colossal, 1 year	25	50	3 50
Conover's Colossal, 2 years	40	75	5 00
Barr's M., Palmetto, 1 year	35	75	5 00
Barr's M., Palmetto, 2 years	50	1 00	7 00
Rhubarb—Myatts Linnæus and Victoria, 1 year	1 00	4 00	
Myatts Linnæus and Victoria, 2 years	1 50	6 00	
Horse Radish	35	75	
Sage	35		

Apples.	Each	10	100
Standard, 2 to 3 years, 5 to 7 ft.; 1st class	$0 25	$2 00	$12 00
Standard, 2 to 3 years, 4 to 5 ft.	20	1 50	10 00
Standard, 2 to 3 years, 3 to 4 ft.	15	1 20	8 00
Alexander, Wolf River, Yellow Transparent, 5 to 7 ft.	30	2 00	15 00
Alexander, Wolf River, Yellow Transparent, 4 to 5 ft.	25	1 75	12 00
Crab Apples, 2 to 3 years, 5 to 7 ft., first class	30	2 00	
Crab Apples, 2 to 3 years, 4 to 5 ft.	25	1 75	
Dwarf Apples	50	3 50	
Pears.			
Standard, 5 to 7 ft., 1st class	40	3 00	25 00
" 4 to 5 ft.	35	2 50	20 00
" 3 to 4 ft.	30	2 00	16 00
Idaho, & Wilder, 5 to 7 ft.	60	5 00	
" " 4 to 5 ft.	50	4 00	
" " 3 to 4 ft.	40	3 00	
Dwarf, 3 to 4 ft.	30	2 25	15 00
Dwarf, 2 to 3 ft.	25	1 75	12 00
Quinces.			
Angiers, 3 to 4 ft.	35	2 50	
Angiers, 2 to 3 ft.	25	2 00	
Orange and Champion, 3 to 4 ft.	40	3 00	25 00
Orange and Champion, 2 to 3 ft.	30	2 50	20 00
Meech's Prolific and Rea's Mammoth, 3 to 4 ft.	50	4 00	
Meech's Prolific and Rea's Mammoth, 2 to 3 ft.	40	3 00	
Cherries.			
Sweet Varieties, 5 to 7 ft. 1st class	40	3 00	25 00
Sweet Varieties, 4 to 5 ft.	35	2 50	20 00
Sour Varieties, 4 to 5 ft. 1st class.	40	3 00	25 00
Sour Varieties, 3 to 4 ft.	35	2 50	20 00
Plums.			
On Plum roots, 5 to 7 ft.	40	3 00	25 00
On Plum roots, 4 to 5 ft.	35	2 50	20 00
On Plum roots, 3 to 4 ft.	30	2 00	16 00
Abundance, Moore's Arctic, Simons, 5 to 7 ft.	60	5 00	40 00
Abundance, Moore's Arctic, Simons, 4 to 5 ft.	50	4 00	30 00
Abundance, Moore's Arctic, Simons, 3 to 4 ft.	40	3 00	25 00
Peaches.			
4 to 5 ft, 1 year, first-class	20	1 60	12 00
3 to 4 ft, 1 year	15	1 25	10 00
2 to 3 ft, 1 year	12	1 00	8 00
Crosby and Champion at ½ additional to above prices.			

Apricots and Nectarines.	Each	Per 10	Per 100
4 to 5 ft...................	$0 25	$2 00	$15 00
3 to 4 ft...................	20	1 60	12 00
2 to 3 ft,..................	15	1 25	10 00

Nut Trees.			
Almonds, hard and soft shelled, 3 to 4 ft...............	35	2 50	
Butternuts, 4 to 5 ft.........	35	2 50	
Butternuts, 3 to 4 ft..........	25	1 50	
Chestnut, American, 4 to 5 ft...	40	3 00	
Chestnut, American, 3 to 4 ft...	30	2 00	
Chestnut, Japan, 1½ to 2 ft....	50	4 00	
Chestnut, Spanish, 2 to 3 ft..	40	3 00	
Filberts, English, 3 to 4 ft.....	40	3 00	
Hickory, Shellbark, 3 to 4 ft...	40	3 00	
Hickory, Pecan, 2 to 3 ft......	30	2 00	
Walnut, Black, 4 to 5 ft........	50	4 00	
Walnut, English, 2 to 3 ft......	50	4 00	

Mulberries.	Each	Per 10	Per 100
Downing's Everbearing, 5 to 7 ft..	$0 60	$5 00	
Downing's Everbearing, 4 to 5 ft..	50	4 00	
Downing's Everbearing, 3 to 4 ft..	40	3 00	
Russian, 5 to 7 ft.............	35	2 50	
Russian, 4 to 5 ft.............	25	2 00	
Russian, 3 to 4 ft.............	20	1 50	

Dwarf Juneberries,			
2 to 3 ft...................	25	2 00	$15 00

Figs.			
Brown Turkey and Celestial, 1½ to 2 ft....................	40	3 00	

Eleagnus.			
Longipes, 1 year.............	30		
Longipes, 2 year.............	40		

ORNAMENTAL DEPARTMENT.

Deciduous Trees.	Each	Per 10	Per 100		Each	Per 10	Per 100
AILANTHUS—Gland, 5 to 6 ft...	$0 50	$	$	JUDUS TREE—American, 4 to 5 ft	$0 50	$	
ALDER—Imp. Cut-l'v'd, 5 to 7 ft	50			LABURNUM—Common, 4 to 5 ft..	50		
European, 5 to 6 ft.........	50			LARCH—European, 3 to 4 ft....	50		
ASH—Acuba-leaved, 4 to 5 ft...	75			LINDEN—American, 5 to 7 ft....	50	4 00	
White and European, 5 to 7 ft.	50	4 00		European, 5 to 7 ft.........	50	4 00	
BALM OF GILEAD—5 to 7 ft....	50			Silver-leaved, 5 to 7 ft........	75		
BEECH—Purple-leaved, 3 to 4 ft	75			LIQUID AMBER—Sweet Gum, 5 to 6 ft....................	50		
Rivers Purple-leaved, 4 to 5 ft	1 00						
Fern-leaved, 3 to 4 ft........	1 00			MAGNOLIA—Acuminata (Cucumber tree), 4 to 5 ft..........	50		
European, 3 to 4 ft.........	75			Acuminata, 5 to 7 ft........	75		
BIRCH—Pyramidalis, 5 to 7 ft...	50	4 00		Speciosa, 2 to 3 ft...........	1 00		
Pyramidalis, 8 to 10 ft.......	75	6 00		Soulangiana, 2 to 3 ft........	1 00		
CATALPA—Bungei, 6 to 7 ft....	1 00			MAPLE—Silver-leaved, 5 to 7 ft..	40	3 00	
Speciosa, 6 to 8 ft..........	50	4 00		Silver-leaved, 7 to 9 ft.......	50	4 00	
Speciosa, 8 to 10 ft..........	75	6 00		Norway, 5 to 7 ft...........	75	6 00	
Teas Japan, 6 to 8 ft........	50	4 00		Schwedlerii, 4 to 6 ft.......	1 00		
Teas Japan, 8 to 10 ft.......	75	6 00		Wier's Cut-leaved, 5 to 6 ft....	40	3 60	
CORNUS— (Dogwood) —White Flowering, 3 to 4 ft......,	50			Wier's Cut-leaved, 6 to 8 ft....	50	4 00	
Red Flowering, 2½ to 3 ft....	75			MOUNTAIN ASH—Eu., 5 to 7 ft...	40	3 00	
ELM—American White, 5 to 7 ft	50	4 00		European, 7 to 9 ft.........	50	4 00	
American White, 8 to 10 ft...	75	6 00		Oak-leaved, 5 to 6 ft.........	50	4 00	
Scotch and Red, 5 to 7 ft....	60	5 00		OAK—Cork-bark, 5 to 7 ft......	75		
Scotch and Red, 8 to 10 ft....	75	6 00		Scarlet, 4 to 5 ft............	75		
EUNONYMUS)European Strawberry Tree)—5 to 7 ft.....	40			OLIVE—Russian, 3 to 4 ft......	50		
3½ to 5 ft................	25			POPLAR—Lombardy, 6 to 8 ft....	30	2 50	
HORSE CHESTNUT—White flowering, 4 to 5 ft.............	50			Lombardy, 8 to 10 ft........	40	3 50	
Double White, 4 to 5 ft......	1 00			Golden-leaved, 8 to 10 ft......	40	3 50	
Red flowering, 4 to 5 ft......	1 00			Carolina, 6 to 8 ft..........	30	2 50	
				Carolina, 8 to 10 ft...........	40	3 50	

	Each	Per 10	Per 100
SALISBURIA—Maiden Hair Tree, 5 to 7 ft............	$0 60	$5 00	$
THORNS—Double white, Pink, Red and Paul's Scarlet, 3 to 4 ft..................	50	4 00	
4 to 5 ft..................	60	5 00	
TULIP TREE—6 to 8 ft......	75		

Weeping Deciduous Trees.

	Each	Per 10	Per 100
ASH—Gold Bark...........	1 00		
BEECH—Pendula, 3 to 4 ft....	1 50		
BIRCH—Cut-leaved, Weeping 5 to 6 ft.............	60	5 00	
6 to 8 ft..............	80	7 00	
Elegans Pendula, 3 to 4 ft...	1 50		
CORNUS—(Dogwood)—Florida Pendula, 2 to 3 ft........	1 00		
ELM—Fulva Pendula, 5 to 7 ft..	1 00		
Camperdown, 1 year heads...	1 00		
LINDEN—White-leaved, 3-4 ft.	75		
MOUNTAIN ASH—Weeping...	75	6 00	
MULBERRY—Teas New Russian, 1 year heads........	1 00		
Teas, New Russian, 2 year heads..................	1 25		
POPLAR—Large-leaved......	1 00		
WILLOW—Kilmarnock, 1 year heads	50	4 00	
Kilmarnock, 2 year heads...	60	5 00	
American new, 1 year heads.	50	4 00	
Babylonica, 5 to 7 ft......	50	4 00	
Wisconsin, 5 to 7 ft.......	50	4 00	

Deciduous Shrubs,

	Each	Per 10	Per 100
ALMOND—Double flowering, 2 to 3 ft................	30		
ALTHEA—(Rose of Sharon)— Double, 4 varieties, 2 to 3 ft.	30	2 50	
Variegated-leaved, 2 to 3 ft..	50	4 00	
AZALEA—Ponticum, 12 to 15 inches	50		
Mollis, 12 to 15 inches......	50		
AMORPHA—Fragrans and Fruiticosa.............	30	2 50	
BERBERRY—European common and purple-leaved, 2 ft.	25	2 00	
European common, 15 to 20 inches	15	1 00	5 00
BUCKTHORN—Purging, 2-3 ft..	30	2 50	15 00
CALYCANTHUS—Flori's, 2-3 ft.	35	3 00	
CORNUS—(Dogwood)—Sanguinea, 3 ft.............	25	2 00	
Elegantissima Var., 2-3 ft...	50		
CORCHORUS—Japonica, 2-3 ft.	25	2 00	
CURRANTS—Crimson and yellow flowering..........	25		
DEUTZIA—Crenata, double flowering, 3 to 4 ft.......	25	2 00	
Gracilis, 12 to 15 inches.....	25	2 00	
EXOCHORDIA—Grandiflora, 2 to 3 ft................	35		

	Each	Per 10	Per 100
EUONYMUS—(Burning Bush),— European, 4 to 5 ft........	$0 40	$3 00	$
ELDER—Cut-leaved, 3 to 4 ft....	50		
Golden-leaved, 2 to 3 ft.......	50		
Variegated-leaved, 2 to 3 ft....	35	3 00	
FILBERT—Purple-leaved, 3 to 4 ft	50		
FORSYTHIA—(Golden Bell)—Viridisma, 3 to 4 ft............	25	2 00	
FRINGE—Purple [smoke tree], 3 to 4 ft..................	40	3 00	
White, 2 to 3 ft............	50		
HONEYSUCKLE—Tartarian, Red and White, 2 to 3 ft.........	25	2 00	
HYDRANGIA—Paniculata Grandiflora 18 to 24 inches.......	25	2 00	
Paniculata Grand, 2 to 3 ft....	35	3 00	
LILAC—White and Purple, 3 to 4 ft.....................	25	2 00	
Japan Tree, new, 5 to 6 ft.....	1 00		
PHILADELPHUS [Mock Orange] Large flowered, 3 to 4 ft....	25	2 00	
Double flowered, 2 to 3 ft.....	35	2 50	
Golden-leaved, 1½ to 2 ft.....	35	2 50	
PRUNUS PISARDI—Purple-leaved Plum, 3 to 4 ft......	35	3 00	
Triloba, Double flowering Plum, 2 to 3 ft.................	35		
PRIVET—California, 1 to 1½ ft...	15	1 00	5 00
California, 1½ to 2 ft......	20	1 50	8 00
QUINCE—(Pyrus Japonica)— Scarlet, 1 to 2 ft....	25	2 00	10 00
SNOWBERRY—White and Red fruited, 2 to 3 ft............	25	2 00	
SPIREAS—Twelve Varieties, 2 to 3 ft	25	2 00	
Golden-leaved, 2 to 3 ft......	35	3 00	
TAMARIX—Africana, 3 to 4 ft...	25	2 00	
TREE PAEONIES—Banksii, 1 yr.	75	6 00	
Banksii 2 year.............	1 00	8 00	
VIBURNUM—Snowball, 2 to 3 ft.	25	2 00	
Plicatum (Japanese) 1½ to 2 ft.	50		
Highbush Cranberry, 1½ to 2 ft.	40	3 00	
WEIGELIA—In variety, 2 to 3 ft.	25	2 00	
Variegated-leaved, 2 to 3 ft....	30	2 50	
White flowering, 2 to 3 ft......	35	3 00	

Climbing Vines.

	Each	Per 10	Per 100
AMPELOPSIS—American Ivy...	20	1 50	
Veitchii—[Japanese Ivy]......	30	2 50	
ARISTOLOCHIA—Sipho [Dutchman's Pipe]..............	35		
BIGNONIA—[Trumpet Flower]— Radicans, Scarlet..........	25	2 00	
CLEMATIS—Virginica, Flammula, Coccinia, Crispa..........	25	2 00	
Jackmanii, Henryi, Kermisina, etc., 1 year.............	50	4 00	
Jackmanii, Henryi, Kermisina, etc., 2 years..............	75	6 50	
Jackmanii, Henryi, Kermisina, etc., 3 years..............	1 00		

	Each	Per 10	Per 100
HONEYSUCKLE—Scarlet, Trumpet, Halleana, Monthly, Fragrant, etc.	$0 20	$1 50	$
IVY—English	20	1 50	
WISTERIA — Chinese Blue, 2 years	25	2 00	
Chinese White	50		
Double Purple	60		

Evergreen Trees.

	Each	Per 10	Per 100
ARBOR VITÆ—American, 8 to 12 inches	20	1 00	4 00
American, 12 to 18 inches	25	2 00	7 00
American, 2 to 3 ft	50	4 00	16 00
Hovey's Golden, 18 to 24 inches	50	3 00	
Siberian, 1 to 2 ft	50		
Tom Thumb, 12 to 15 inches	50		
FIR, SILVER — American Balsam, 2 to 3 ft	50	4 00	
Frazerii, 12 to 15 inches	50		
Nordmaniana, 15 to 18 inches	75		
JUNIPER—Irish, 2 to 3 in	75	6 00	
Virginia (Red Cedar) 2 to 3 feet	75	6 00	
PINE—Austrian, 2 to 3 ft	50	4 00	30 00
Austrian, 12 to 15 inches	30	2 00	15 00
Montana Dwarf, 15 to 18 in	50	4 00	
Scotch, 1½ to 2 ft	50	4 00	
White, 1½ to 2 ft	50	4 00	
RETINOSPORA—Plumosa, 2 to 3 feet	50		
Plumosa Aurea, 2 to 3 ft	75		
SPRUCE—Norway, 12 to 15 in	25	2 00	6 00
Norway, 2 to 3 feet	40	3 00	18 00
Hemlock, 12 to 18 inches	40	3 00	20 00
Colorado Blue, 12 to 15 inches	1 00		
YEW—Ellegantisima, 15 to 20 in.	1 00		
Irish, 15 to 20 inches	1 00		

Evergreen Shrubs.

	Each	Per 10	Per 100
ASHBERY—(Mahonia) Holly-leaved, 1 to 1½ feet	40		
AZALEA — Amœnea, 12 to 15 inches	50		
BOX—(Buxus) Tree Box, 8 to 12 inches	25	2 00	
Tree Box, Variegated, 6 to 10 inches	35		
Dwarf Box, 4 to 6 inches	10	60	4 00
HOLLY—Silver Queen, 6 to 10 in.	1 00		
English, 10 to 12 inches	35		
RHODODENDRONS — Catawbiense Seedlings, 12 inches	1 00		
Catawbiense Seedling, 2 feet	1 50		
Choice Grafted Varieties, 1½ feet	1 50		
Choice Grafted Varieties, 2 ft	2 00		

Roses.

	Each	Per 10	Per 100
HYBRID PERPETUALS—2 years	$0 30	$2 50	$
CLIMBING—2 years	30	2 50	
CLIMBING — Gem of Prairie, 2 years	35	3 00	
MOSS—2 years	30	2 50	

Hedge Plants.

	Each	Per 10	Per 100
OSAGE ORANGE—1 year, per 1000 $3 00			50
OSAGE ORANGE—2 years, per 1000, $4 00			65
HONEY LOCUST—1 year, per 1000 $5 00			75
HONEY LOCUST—2 years, yer 1000 $7 50			1 00

See also Berberry, Quince and Privet among Deciduous Shrubs. Also Arbor Vitæ, Spruce and Juniper among Evergreens.

Hardy Plants and Bulbs.

	Each	Per 10	Per 100
Achillea, Anemonic Japonica, Alba and Rubra, Astilbes, Delphinium, Dicentra Dictamus, Eulalie Zebrina and Variegata, Funkia Alba, Helianthus, Hollyhocks, Iris, Phlox assortment, Tritoma Uvaria, Yucca Filamentosa	20	1 50	
LILIES—Auratum (Gold Banded.) Speciosum, Rubrum and Roseum	25	2 00	
Speciosum Album	35		
Lily of the Valley	10	50	3 00
Pæonies in variety	25	2 00	

Tender Bulbs and Tubers.

	Each	Per 10	Per 100
Caladium Escul	15	1 20	
Cannas, 10 varieties	15	1 00	
Cannas, choice Dwarf French	20	1 50	
Dahlias, fine assortment	25	2 00	
Gladiolus, mixed, fine	10	60	3 00
Gladiolus, named varieties	15	1 00	6 00
Madeira Vines, Tigridia and Tuberoses	10	60	3 00

CPSIA information can be obtained
at www.ICGtesting.com
Printed in the USA
BVHW04*0946210918
527831BV00034B/1025/P